RELUCTANT MANAGERS

November
194

RELUCTANT MANAGERS

Their Work and Lifestyles

Richard Scase & Robert Goffee

London and New York

First published 1989
by the Academic Division of Unwin Hyman Ltd

Reprinted 1993
by Routledge
11 New Fetter Lane, London EC4P 4EE
29 West 35th Street, New York, NY 10001

Typeset in 10½ on 13 point Bembo by Nene Phototypesetters Ltd.
Printed and bound in Great Britain by
Biddles Ltd, Guildford and King's Lynn

British Library Cataloguing in Publication Data
A catalogue record for this book is available from the British Library

ISBN 0-415-08466-0 (pbk)

Library of Congress Cataloging-in-Publication Data has been applied for

ISBN 0-415-08466-0 (pbk)

Contents

Preface		*page* vii
1	The changing context of work, careers and lifestyles	1
2	The costs and benefits of work	20
3	Organizational change and management style	53
4	Personal ambitions and careers	78
5	Women, work and careers	106
6	Home lives and personal lifestyles	129
7	Men and women managers and their partners	155
8	Conclusions	179
	Methodological appendix	192
	Bibliography	199
	Index	210

Preface

In this book we attempt to describe the work and lifestyles of men and women managers as they reported them to us in a variety of work and home settings. We have deliberately chosen to present and discuss these in relatively non-theoretical terms so that practising managers and non-academics should find the book reasonably straightforward and uncomplicated.

We are grateful to the Economic and Social Research Council for funding the research upon which this book is based and to Jane Benson who, as research assistant, helped us to collect much of the data. We would like to thank Jan and Ray Pahl for encouraging us to look again at the lifestyles of managers and our colleagues Phillip Brown at the University of Kent and Gareth Jones and John Hunt at London Business School for their comments on earlier drafts. Above all, however, we are appreciative of the co-operation given to us by the men and women managers who, employed in six large organizations, took part in the study. This book is for them and their partners.

Richard Scase and Robert Goffee

CHAPTER 1

The changing context of work, careers and lifestyles

The growth of management and large-scale organizations during the twentieth century has been one of the more significant features of modern society. In all Western countries, amalgamations and takeovers have led to the emergence of corporations that dominate not only local and national economies but also determine the nature of trading relationships in the international marketplace (Hannah, 1975; Hannah and Kay, 1977; Scott, 1986; Utton, 1970). Indeed, despite recent programmes of privatization and the present-day political popularity of market competition, most national states have expanded the provision of their central and local services in such areas as education, health and social welfare (Davis and Scase, 1985; Scase, 1980). It is, then, hardly surprising that the increasing influence and, indeed, dominance of large-scale institutions, bureaucracies and privately owned corporations have attracted the interest of economists, political scientists and sociologists.[1] The emergence of such organizations raises important issues about patterns of decision-making in society, the ownership and control of economic, political and social resources, and the extent to which they are sufficiently publicly accountable and socially responsible (Galbraith, 1967; Illich, 1975; Kumar, 1989). At the same time, their structure and design have posed many questions for those interested in organizational 'efficiency' and how far these are appropriate for attaining explicitly stated goals.[2]

[1]

Within large-scale organizations, human, technical and financial resources have to be co-ordinated and controlled. In addition, work tasks need to be defined and allocated to individuals whose job performance must be supervised and measured. In short, organizations must be *managed* and, as such, the responsibility for this rests with those who, within the context of different organizational settings, are variously designated as managers.[3] Thus, the growth of large-scale organizations has witnessed the appearance of management as a central organizational activity. Indeed, as a reflection of this and their general control of organizational resources, managers have traditionally been highly rewarded, in terms not only of their salaries and fringe benefits but also in their status and working conditions (Poole *et al.*, 1981; Routh, 1980).[4] But how do they perceive and interpret their work roles? Despite their relatively privileged positions, how far are managers committed to their jobs and employing organizations? To what extent are changes occurring both in their work settings and in the wider society which are reducing many of their customary benefits? During the closing decades of the twentieth century, many public sector institutions and privately owned corporations are reviewing their operating practices, redesigning jobs, and reassessing the effectiveness of their structures in response to rapidly changing external and internal circumstances (Handy, 1984; Kanter, 1983). Accordingly, like most other employees, managers are likely to be more rigorously appraised and, as a result, more prone to occupational risk and redundancy (Berthoud, 1979; Wood and Dey, 1983). Their jobs, careers and employment prospects are characterized by greater uncertainties and these, in turn, are likely to be having important implications for their attitudes and personal lifestyles. In this book we discuss how men and women managers are responding to such changes.

Generally speaking, studies of managers are often limited in their perspectives. There is a tendency for discussions to concentrate narrowly upon how they perform their work tasks and to neglect the ways in which their roles are shaped

[2]

by various organizational processes and broader social and economic forces.[5] There are few attempts to understand how managerial practices *within* organizations can be conditioned by *outside* factors which influence the ways in which, for example, different patterns of decision-making and leadership style become widely regarded as appropriate for obtaining operating efficiency. Styles of management which are considered as effective at one point in time may cease to be seen as such when prevailing values and assumptions change during a subsequent era.[6] Managers in the 1980s, then, are often expected to adopt work practices and use incentive schemes which are quite different from those recommended as suitable during the 1950s and 1960s (Bowey, 1982; White, 1981). In the intervening period, various economic, technological and social changes have not only altered the internal dynamics of organizations but also the environments within which they operate.

During the immediate postwar decades, economic growth facilitated the expansion of business corporations and state-owned institutions. Managers at this time could be reasonably optimistic about their career prospects and, in turn, their opportunities for enjoying steadily improving living standards (Gans, 1967; Whyte, 1965). Most expected to be both occupationally and geographically mobile and were prepared to accept the associated costs for their personal lifestyles and family relationships (Bell, 1968; Watson, 1964). These were seen as the price which had to be paid for the rewards of successful careers. According to several observers, managers belonged to an affluent and rapidly expanding middle class which, in turn, was the product of a 'new', more 'open' society within which academic, technical and professional forms of meritocratic qualification were gaining ascendancy over more traditional forms of hereditary class privilege (Aron, 1967; Lipset and Bendix, 1959; Young, 1961). Such changes were proclaimed by some as bringing about the demise of capitalist society. The increasing predominance of large-scale organizations and the growth of state intervention

[3]

and planning were, they argued, creating a different social order which could more appropriately be described as 'post-capitalist' (Bell, 1974; Dahrendorf, 1959).[7] As such, new forms of social stability were replacing 'old-fashioned' class divisions and antagonistic political ideologies. Large-scale public and private sector organizations, often characterized as technostructures, were seen as central to the fabric of this emerging socio-economic order, and those employed within them – managers, professionals and other highly-qualified technical employees – were expected to be committed to values and ideologies which emphasized the 'common good' (Galbraith, 1967). They embodied, in other words, the 'classless' attitudes and lifestyles alleged to characterize the postwar consensus. As 'organization men' – there were very few women managers – they were expected to subscribe to work values which gave priority to corporate demands over other interests, including those of personal relationships and lifestyles (Whyte, 1965). Personal identity and self-worth were assumed to be overwhelmingly derived from occupational and career accomplishments (Glaser and Strauss, 1971; Sofer, 1970).

During the 1950s and 1960s, then, the careers and lifestyles of managers were seen to reflect the predominant ideals and assumptions of postwar society. In many ways, their achievements and rewards set the standards or models which others were encouraged to emulate. It was not until the late 1960s that many of these prevailing views were challenged.[8] Opposition came mainly from university and college students who were, themselves, the product of middle-class affluence and who had witnessed, at first hand, the career successes of their parents (Brake, 1985). These young people offered alternative interpretations of their parents' achievements. Whereas, for example, their fathers regarded profit-making corporations as vehicles for economic progress and improved living standards, they viewed them as purveyors of 'false values'. For them the 'rational' pursuit of profit led to the 'irrational' use of natural resources, to pollution and to ecological destruction (Dickson, 1974; Ellul, 1975).[9] At the same time, the 'affluent' society was seen to foster ideals which negated the development of human potential and creativity (Marcuse, 1964). Accordingly, career success was seen to be 'meaningless' because it produced rewards that were solely materialistic. Whereas their parents saw modern corporations as offering opportunities for personal success, they regarded them with suspicion since they appeared to dictate how individuals should think and behave within and beyond the workplace. Some deliberately cultivated 'alternative', 'hippy' lifestyles which stood in sharp contrast to the conventional and rational behaviour required of their fathers as corporate executives (Reich, 1970; Abrams and McCulloch, 1976).

The wider implications of career pursuit for family and other personal relations became increasingly the focus of attention in the late 1960s as managers' emotional relationships with their wives and children became recognized as more distant (Whyte, 1965; Seeley, Sim and Lossely, 1963). At the same time, there was a growing awareness of the problems encountered by their wives, whose feelings of psychological and material dependence were reinforced by social pressures which inhibited any aspirations they may have had for independent careers (Pahl and Pahl, 1971; Gavron, 1968). Thus, although the re-emergent women's movement initially appealed primarily to university students, it gained some support among younger, married middle-class women who, albeit educationally qualified and with high work aspirations, were unable to sustain their own careers because of traditional assumptions that these should be subordinated to those of their husbands (Mitchell, 1971). Their frustrations led them to query many of the values underlying middle-class conjugal relationships and encouraged them to challenge the ways in which their husbands' career pursuits reinforced their own domestic and subordinate identities.

However, despite questioning certain aspects of their

middle-class work roles and lifestyles, managers and their wives remained predominantly satisfied with their opportunities and rewards. Although their university and college educated children may have expressed reservations about prevailing ideals this did not prevent them from seeking jobs which offered high salaries and promising career prospects. Some may have briefly 'opted out' or retained their affiliation to radical political parties but, on the whole, the majority proceeded to pursue relatively conventional career strategies within the confines of private and public sector organizations. Equally, those managers' wives who may have queried many of the established views concerning their expected social roles, continued to enjoy the material rewards derived from their husbands' career success (Finch, 1983). There is little evidence that many declined to take holidays abroad, to enjoy the advantages of 'second' cars and the comforts of large and well-equipped houses! In other words, their lifestyles and personal status continued to be dependent upon their husbands' career success. Such rewards, they and their husbands claimed, were available to all who were ambitious, were prepared to work hard and wished to succeed in the more open, achievement-oriented society of postwar Britain (Pahl and Pahl, 1971).

It is not surprising that much of the political debate during the 1960s was concerned with issues to do with 'classlessness', 'affluence' and 'equality' (Zweig, 1961). While more socially concerned politicians addressed themselves to the problems of public squalor in an age of private affluence, sociologists and political scientists were engaged in debates about the 'embourgeoisement' of the so-called newly affluent working class (Goldthorpe et al., 1969). Such trends were also of interest to the growing numbers of town planners, architects, teachers and social workers who felt increasingly responsible for state-sponsored projects intended to modernize Britain's social, economic and material fabric (Jessop, 1980). The 1960s witnessed a rapid growth of the welfare state and, with it, the expansion of a variety of associated institutional structures. These, in turn, offered new and increasing career and job prospects for managers, professionals and different technical experts. They also created the need for public sector management as a specialist function with its own specific principles and codes of practice.[10] Even so, like their colleagues in large, privately owned corporations, these managers worked within hierarchies where pay, promotion, security and the associated incremental enhancements in status and responsibility were major incentives. Managers in both public and private sectors, then, derived satisfaction from their jobs in so far as these were located within clearly defined career structures where personal progress could be measured according to age, experience and achievement. Such similarities in their work and organizational experiences helped to shape common, socio-political attitudes and values. These emphasized the desirability of 'state intervention' and the 'mixed economy' for the purposes of achieving economic growth and for raising living standards which, in turn, were reflected in the predominant assumptions of both the Conservative and Labour parties (Poole et el., 1981). Such a 'middle way', established as it was upon a postwar political consensus, stressed the desirability of socio-economic planning so that *both* economic efficiency and the provision of collective welfare would be enhanced. In order to operate effectively, it was argued, this planning required interdependent technostructures located within both public and private sectors. Accordingly, the mixed economy of the postwar decades possessed the core features of what has subsequently become known as 'corporatism' (Goldthorpe, 1984; McCrone, Elliott and Bechhofer, 1989; Strinati, 1982).

Such were the prevailing trends of the 1950s and 1960s. If during the latter part of this period certain middle-class values and assumptions became subject to query they were the focus of further challenge during the 1970s. Feelings of optimism and self-confidence were superseded by a growing pessimism as many managers realized that their career ambitions and aspirations for improved living standards would be unful-

[7]

filled (Elliot and McCrone, 1987). A number of factors contributed to this but, on reflection, three would seem to be particularly pertinent. First, the early 1970s witnessed a significant change in the climate of industrial relations in Britain. There was an increase in the level of disputes while, at the same time, full employment enabled organized labour to maintain a strong bargaining position in its negotiations with management (Crouch, 1977; Hyman, 1972). For many, the coalminers' strike in 1974, and the miners' ability to obtain important concessions from the Conservative government, symbolized the 'excessive' influence of trade unionism (Goffee, 1976). Accordingly, there was much debate as to whether corporate managers were any longer capable of exercising control at the workplace (Purcell and Sissons, 1983). Secondly, the 'oil crisis' in 1973 not only increased the production costs of manufacturing concerns, but also weakened the competitive position of the British economy as a whole, organized as it was on the availability of cheap energy resources (Jackson, 1974). Finally, a rapid increase in the rate of inflation during the latter part of the decade eroded living standards, personal savings and, indeed, the self-confidence of the middle class (King and Nugent, 1979). Such developments challenged the underlying assumptions of the postwar political consensus which had given priority to economic planning, the virtues of the mixed economy and corporatism.[11] This culminated in the defeat of the Labour Party in 1979 and the election of a Conservative government committed to reforming industrial relations and to restructuring the economy. Thus, many of the mechanisms of corporatism have been abandoned, state intervention in industry reduced and companies encouraged to be efficient by 'independently' trading in national and international markets rather than through collaborative 'modernizing' projects with government (McCrone, Elliott and Bechhofer, 1989).

With the election of successive Conservative governments in the 1980s, members of the middle class might be expected to have regained their self-confidence. Politically, they may

have done so. However, government economic and industrial strategies committed to radical reforms are, both directly
and indirectly, subjecting many to greater demands in their
working lives. As both public and private sector organizations are forced to become more 'cost effective' and
'efficient', managers are being increasingly pressurized to
demonstrate their competence and to achieve higher levels of
measurable performance (Regional Reward Surveys, 1985).
Demands for greater efficiency often mean that they can no
longer be assured of relatively secure jobs with reasonably
predictable career prospects (Handy, 1984; Thackray, 1986;
Toffler, 1985). Like other employees, they are subject to
corporate restructuring such that the nature of their jobs and
the duties which they are expected to perform are frequently
redesigned, changed and abolished. Even those corporations
which have expanded their trading activities during this
period have often done so without needing to increase their
staff levels.[12] In many cases, this has been achieved by
implementing strategies geared more to the production and/
or sale of products and services for specialist rather than more
general markets.[13] Consequently, organizational restructuring has led to the increased adoption of smaller specialist,
wholly owned subsidiaries and 'strategic business units'.
Further, corporate strategies are now more likely to be
concerned with achieving profits through consolidating and
contracting various trading activities and through divestment
rather than solely through high-volume growth. At the same
time, the application of computer-based information systems
has enabled senior management to cut overheads through
reducing their needs for routine clerical workers and various
categories of junior and middle managers (Jenkins and Sherman, 1979).

The increasing emphasis upon cost reduction has had
important implications for the work roles and careers of
managers. In many organizations, fewer are needed if only
because there are less staff to supervise. Equally, the adoption
of 'flatter', relatively decentralized structures – often made

possible by the application of developments in computerized technology – has resulted in a reduction in the size and extent of management hierarchies (Buchanan and Boddy, 1983). Further, managers' anxieties about redundancy have been reinforced by the ways in which macroeconomic changes have brought about not only the collapse of some well-established companies but also an increase in the incidence of corporate mergers and takeovers (Hunt *et al.*, 1987).[14] Thus, the subsequent 'rationalization' of productive systems in manufacturing companies and of sales outlets in retailing has often reduced the need for managerial and other supervisory staff and even those who are not directly affected by such schemes are likely to have considerable doubts about their *potential* vulnerability.[15]

In line with these processes, there has been a reappraisal of the validity of traditional bureaucratic models of management practice (Mintzberg, 1979). Until recently, there was a widely-held view that organizations should consist of precisely defined roles of authority and accountability within relatively centralized operating structures.[16] It was argued that organizations of this kind were efficient because they enabled staff to increase their competences through the performance of their various specialized skills. At the same time, through the precise delineation of strategies and procedures, such organizations could, it was argued, achieve their goals more effectively than those that were less bureaucratically structured. Perhaps, in relatively stable market conditions, such organizations can achieve their goals with the minimum degree of operational ambiguity and uncertainty. At the same time, they can offer highly visible incentives to staff by rewarding them with promotion in clearly defined career structures. However, in more dynamic and uncertain environmental circumstances the applicability of the bureaucratic model is subject to query. It is becoming increasingly recognized that large-scale organizations, in both the private and public sectors, must be more adaptive and, hence, more flexible in their operating procedures. Further,

[10]

in highly competitive markets, overheads must be kept to a minimum and conditions established whereby innovation and change can be encouraged (Kanter, 1983). Consequently, there are now frequent attempts to develop 'looser' forms of organization through reducing their dependency upon rules and fixed procedures (Peters, 1988). Instead of rewarding managers with security and relatively orderly career progression there are now greater attempts to offer incentives through various performance-related incentive schemes. Working relationships are encouraged to be informal and flexible within open communication networks, the structures of which are varied according to the changing nature of stipulated goals (Pinchot, 1985). Thus, the dependency upon formalized structures is minimized and, through the cultivation of 'high trust' relationships, senior managers in many corporations are attempting to reduce costs through abolishing lower-level managerial tiers (Nichols and Beynon, 1977). As mechanisms of organizational integration, these are supposed to enable senior managers to minimize their dependency upon rules and formalized procedures as means for co-ordinating and controlling their staff (Peters and Waterman, 1982; Stewart, 1986). As such, they hope to gain greater organizational flexibility, lower operating costs, and improved opportunities for enhancing the commitment and motivation of their junior managerial staff.

Changes of this kind can have important repercussions for the nature of managerial work roles. There are now greater needs for managers to cope with operational uncertainties, and attempts to abolish management tiers through the creation of 'flatter' structures can lead to more restricted career opportunities than those available in more highly structured settings. Hence, managers are often required to develop more adaptive or flexible interpersonal skills of the kinds which are not sanctioned in more bureaucratic structures. Indeed, coupled with such changes it is frequently argued that managerial careers are becoming less confined to a single or a limited number of organizations but, instead, are character-

[11]

ized by a variety of employment experiences. Accordingly, it is often claimed that more managers will be forced to make more frequent moves between jobs, often becoming self-employed and, indeed, redundant (Handy, 1984). Those who become self-employed may 'sell back' their services to previous employers and, often, be compelled to acquire new skills.[17] If as corporate managers they supervised others, as self-employed consultants they have to be experienced as negotiators and capable of being more entrepreneurial in their attitudes (Scase and Goffee, 1986; 1987). If they become more mobile between companies, their long-term commitment to any single employer is likely to diminish. Perhaps, more so than in the past, they may be compelled to develop personal talents and technical skills which are transferable to a number of different organizational settings (Nicholson and West, 1988). It is for such reasons that observers have argued that managers will be more likely to pursue 'occupational' rather than 'organizational' careers (Brown, 1982; Crompton and Sanderson, 1986). They will need to acquire a variety of interpersonal skills which can be used within a variety of organizational contexts.

If, according to some writers, the work experiences of managers could be changing in these ways, others argue that their job tasks are becoming more precisely defined, closely monitored and tightly regulated (Gallie, 1978; Child, 1984; Mintzberg, 1979). In more bureaucratic forms, the application of computer-based information systems may enable senior managers to exercise tighter control over their subordinates and measure their performance more precisely (Buchanan and Boddy, 1983). As a result, it can be argued that there are tendencies which are polarizing the structure of modern management. On the one hand, there are those senior managers who are able to enjoy considerable autonomy and discretion in their jobs; on the other, there are growing numbers of middle and junior managers whose tasks are becoming 'de-skilled' as their work duties become more precisely defined and subject to tighter forms of

[12]

supervisory control. Indeed, even within those organizations which are restructuring there may be an emerging paradox. If the creation of non-bureaucratic structural forms is *explicitly* intended to extend working autonomy to lower-level managers, the introduction of performance-related rewards often makes them, at the same time, *more directly accountable* to senior managers who set the targets and determine overall strategy (Child, 1984). As such, the commitment, motivation and job satisfaction of middle and junior managers may be severely eroded as they become even more excluded from participation in the decision-making processes surrounding the specification of major corporate objectives.

If, in earlier decades, managers were committed to their jobs to the extent that all other interests were subordinated to their work-related goals, they may be now developing more *instrumental* and *calculative* attitudes towards their employing organizations (Hearn, 1977). Indeed, by deliberately cultivating personal identities that are separate and removed from organizational demands, they could be better equipped to cope with work-related stresses and to withstand the psychological challenges that can be posed by threats of redundancy and unexpected career changes. Accordingly, managers may cease to be *psychologically immersed* in their work roles and become less committed to their employing organizations. To do otherwise, in the light of increasing uncertainties, would be to make themselves more emotionally and psychologically vulnerable.[18]

Such attitudes are reinforced by the recognition that an excessive commitment to occupational success can be severely 'dehumanizing'. If, in order to be effective, managers need to be relatively impersonal and non-emotional in their conduct towards others, such attributes may inhibit their potential for maintaining close intimate relationships outside work. Accordingly, this could be encouraging many of them to reassess the emotional and psychological costs of career success (Evans and Bartolomé, 1980). As such, they are more inclined to define their jobs in almost solely instrumental,

[13]

non-affective terms; as sources of income for achieving self-fulfilment outside employment. Work for large numbers of them, then, acquires meaning comparable to that experienced by many other occupational groups. It ceases to offer important psychological rewards and no longer acts as the pivot around which non-work activities and personal relationships are organized. Indeed, it could be that this kind of reappraisal is most apparent among middle-level, middle-aged, 'plateaued' managers (Hunt and Collins, 1983).

Evidence of the emergence of these feelings is reflected in the growing popularity of early retirement schemes among older managers (McGoldrick, 1983). Indeed, some have argued that the time span of managerial careers has been reduced over recent years (Handy, 1984). In some large organizations, managers are increasingly encouraged to prepare for retirement by their mid-50s (Handy, 1983). This is in sharp contrast with the earlier postwar decades when many of them could expect to be employed after normal retirement age. Thus, a possible consequence of such a trend could be that their organizational commitment declines at an earlier age since, by their early 50s, they are beginning to anticipate non-work futures. Hence, the alleged 'mid-career crises' which many managers are supposed to experience may be acquiring a new significance. If, in the past, it was associated with dramatic shifts in work and career preferences, it may now also lead to plans for early retirement. Of course, such decisions are likely to be shaped by a variety of factors including family responsibilities and the employment prospects of spouses, but it could be argued that their commitment to work is now more compressed within a much reduced time span and may occur within a shorter period during their 30s. If, during their 20s, they are moving between companies and obtaining different work experiences, by their 40s they are beginning to become less career oriented.

This reassessment of the priority of work in personal lifestyles may well have been precipitated by the growth of the womens' movement and the associated changes in women's expectations about employment and the nature of marital relationships (Oakley, 1982; Finch, 1983; Goffee and Scase, 1985). Male managers can now less easily assume that their partners will be prepared to make sacrifices in order to help them in their careers. Married women are more likely to resist house moves associated with their husbands' promotion if this entails their having to relinquish their own jobs, careers and other interests. If the 'organization men' of the past could assume the support of their wives in their pursuit of careers, this appears less likely to be the case today. Middle-class women, in particular, are more inclined to cultivate their own separate identities which are linked to independent work, career and leisure activities (Marshall, 1984; Rapoport and Rapoport, 1976). The appeal of reflecting their husbands' career success through their own 'conspicuous consumption' has probably diminished; at least, to a certain extent.[19] At the same time, the broader impact of feminist ideas has encouraged many women to develop their own talents and to be more assertive in their lifestyles and personal relationships. Further, an increase in the frequency of 'dual career' and 'dual income' families has led many of them to question the value of subordinating their own work interests and lifestyles to those of their husbands. Consequently, the work and career ambitions of men are now more likely to be assessed in terms of the potential *benefits* and *costs* for other family members and for personal relationships. Middle-class family patterns, then, may now offer fewer supports for men's career ambitions than in the past. Indeed, marriage partners can no longer reasonably assume their relationships will be either long-term or permanent. Increases in divorce rates mean that men managers are less able to rely upon the 'uninterrupted' support of their wives, despite the high incidence of remarriage. Accordingly, as men find themselves advised to retain 'emotional energy' for their marriages, they are encouraged to limit the extent of their psychological commitment to their jobs. Their career

[15]

orientations, then, may be a function of the need to restructure personal priorities because of changing expectations about the nature of domestic roles.

However, not all managers are men. Although most are, there has been an increase in the number of women who have become managers during the 1980s, albeit at middle and junior levels (Davidson and Cooper, 1983; Nicholson and West, 1988). In time, this could also have important effects for preferred styles of management. If conventional paradigms have emphasized the need for assertive and non-emotional forms of behaviour – as traditionally associated with 'masculine' qualities in modern Western society – it could be that new, more gender-neutral styles could emerge as more women occupy senior management positions (Marshall, 1984). They could, in these, act as role models, occupational gatekeepers and sponsors of others' careers (Kanter, 1977).[20] However, irrespective of such a trend, it is clear that the changing position of women in employment and within domestic relationships is having significant implications for managerial lifestyles – for both men and women – during the closing decades of the twentieth century.

In this chapter we have briefly reviewed the ways in which organizational restructuring, the emergence of more rapidly changing economies, and the implementation of different forms of 'new' technology are changing the work tasks of many managers' working relationships and personal lifestyles. However, despite the widespread debate of such issues there are remarkably few empirical studies of these processes. In this book we attempt to present a broad overview of some of the major trends. Our evidence is derived from a questionnaire survey and from a series of in-depth interviews which we conducted with men and women managers – together with some of their partners – chosen from six major British organizations. These data offer insights into the changing experiences and attitudes of many present-day managers and, although the survey focuses primarily upon middle managers, they are selected so as to be reasonably 'typical' of wider

[16]

patterns. The inclusion of partners represents an attempt to capture broader non-work experiences and to assess, in particular, the changing interrelationships between work and personal lifestyles. A profile of the managers taking part in our study, together with the organizations from which they are drawn, is provided in the methodological appendix. In order that the presentation of results should be relatively uncomplicated to read, we provide no detailed statistical tables. Instead, we present most of our quantitative data in the form of figures.

Notes

1   The analyses of these processes have been central to both teaching and research in the social sciences in Western societies. Indeed, they have been one of the major reasons why these disciplines have expanded so dramatically during the postwar era.
2   As witnessed in the growth of management science, business studies and various professional and vocationally-related disciplines.
3   The use of the term 'manager' varies considerably from one organizational setting to another. In some it is used to designate levels of status or personal prestige, while in others it delineates a variety of functional responsibilities. We use the term to describe those who, in one way or another, and to varying degrees, co-ordinate and control the behaviour of others.
4   It is interesting that in *all* economies, whether they be capitalist or state socialist, the evidence suggests that 'managers and professionals' are the most highly rewarded groups. A number of theories have been advanced in order to account for this. For a review of some of these see Parkin (1971).
5   This is possibly because of the development of 'organizational behaviour' as a discipline which often, in attempting to distance itself (for one reason or another) from sociology, describes and explains patterns and processes wihin organizations almost entirely to the neglect of broader socio-economic factors.
6   Witness, for instance, the present-day popularity for 'macho' or assertive styles of management which, certainly within the

realm of political rhetoric, are seen to be necessary for reasserting managerial prerogatives.

7 Since capitalism, as a socio-economic order, is organized around the production of goods and services for profit, it is difficult to grasp the distinctiveness of 'post-capitalism' or 'welfare-capitalism' as types of social system, particularly while the profit motive remains central to the wealth creation process.

8 As with many other features of society, the 1960s witnessed the questioning of many cherished middle-class ideals. Much of this had to do with the rapid expansion of institutions of higher education in the Western world and the popularity of the social sciences.

9 The legacy of such ideals has been subsequently reflected in the popularity of 'green' parties in Western Europe which have been able to maintain their support and electoral appeal during the 1980s.

10 It became increasingly recognized that non-profit-making organizations needed to develop their own particular criteria of efficiency and, as such, could not simply imitate the practices and principles of privately-owned corporations.

11 The unexpected emergence of a 'New Right' as a political and rhetorical force offered an appealing agenda of reform to a middle class whose commitment to collectivism, in any case, had been uncertain.

12 Often profit margins have been either maintained or increased through cost-reduction schemes and programmes of 'structural rationalization' which usually lead to staff reductions.

13 'Segmented' rather than 'mass' marketing has become pronounced as companies attempt to carve out more clearly-identifiable trading niches.

14 The underlying motive for many of these is in order to obtain *synergy*. However, in many well-known instances, greater trading effectiveness has not been achieved such that in the 1980s, conglomerates have often 'sold off' those parts of their trading activities which are not regarded as compatible with those of their core ventures.

15 Even the most successful and senior of corporate executives may suddenly find themselves declared 'redundant', after having been instrumental in implementing rationalization programmes.

16 The ideas of F. W. Taylor and the school of thought often

[18]

described as 'scientific management' have been influential in emphasizing the effectiveness of 'mechanistic' models of organization (Morgan, 1986).

17 'Networking' is often used to describe a process whereby companies offer members of their staff voluntary severance and then, on a consultancy basis, 'buy back' their services for particular projects or periods of time.

18 This, of course, can often be the case for those who are forced to take early retirement. Having invested their psychologies into their jobs and having almost exclusively shaped their personal identities around them, they lose all sense of purpose and well-being.

19 The extent to which women who are married to managerial and professional employees develop 'vicarious' identities; that is, self-images derived from their husbands' occupational status has been discussed by Finch (1983).

20 This is already occurring in some entrepreneurial ventures that have been set up by women. Indeed, their motive for start-up is often associated with the desire to escape from the patriarchal nature of large-scale organizations (Goffee and Scase, 1985a).

CHAPTER 2

The costs and benefits of work

In the previous chapter we presented an overview of some of the major economic and social trends which have shaped the experiences of managers over recent decades. This provides the context for a more detailed discussion, in this and the following three chapters, of the ways in which managers' *working* lives are currently changing. Our particular concern is to describe how organizational restructuring and technological change are affecting job expectations, attitudes to work and general feelings of satisfaction. We also consider the relative salience of different kinds of rewards and the extent to which these are being reappraised in the light of organizational and broader socio-economic changes. However, before we can consider these issues in some detail we need to analyse more carefully the nature of managerial work.

Precise specifications are difficult to delineate if only because of the variations in work roles shaped by such factors as functional specialism, level of seniority and organizational context. It is self-evident that the duties and responsibilities of sales managers, for example, differ from those engaged in personnel, production or market research. Equally, senior managers are often engaged in more complex decision-making and negotiation processes than those in positions of junior responsibility (Mintzberg, 1973; Stewart, 1982). Further difficulties derive from the ambiguous and changeable nature of managerial work roles in comparison with, say, the more tightly monitored and clearly-defined jobs of shopfloor and lower-grade, white-collar employees.[1] However, despite these problems, there is considerable

[20]

agreement – from early management theorists, such as Fayol (1949) and Taylor (1947) through to more recent writers as Drucker (1974) – that the 'proper' functions of management should be to *plan* by setting objectives and selecting strategies; to *organize* by delegating and integrating work tasks; to *direct* by leading and motivating staff; and to *control* by monitoring work processes. Contemporary Marxist writers are not dissimilar in their approaches. Carchedi (1975), for example, focuses upon the requirement for managers within different functional specialisms and at varying levels of seniority to undertake two major tasks: those of *co-ordination* and *control*. The first of these is associated with the need to integrate duties in order to implement strategies and to achieve various goals. At the same time, activities in profit-making corporations must be controlled and supervised otherwise the performance required for 'efficiency', 'quality', 'output' and 'profitability' will not be achieved. Consequently, those who do not fulfil the dual tasks of control and co-ordination on a day-to-day basis – for example, professionals and various technical experts who work relatively independently as well as lower-grade administrative and routine white-collar employees – are excluded from such definitions of management. Similarly, in our study, only those who, as part of their jobs, co-ordinate and control the behaviour of others are regarded as managers, and it is these activities rather than those associated with their more technical and specialist functional skills that we focus upon in this chapter.

However, despite the various prescriptions of what managers are *supposed* to do, studies of their actual behaviour suggest they devote only a limited proportion of their time to planning, organizing and goal-setting in an explicit and systematic fashion (Carlson, 1951; Mintzberg, 1973; Stewart, 1982). Further, their efforts to co-ordinate and control are often largely 'reactive' as they respond to apparently unforeseen circumstances and events. So much of their time is devoted to face-to-face encounters, negotiations and meetings that they often claim to be unable to plan and develop long-term strategies (Hunt, 1986). Middle managers, in particular, are subject to conflicting obligations and, in coping with these, they often find that they are preoccupied with routine and technical matters to the neglect of their more managerial responsibilities (Stewart, 1982). At the same time, there are different constraints which vary according to functional specialism as well as level of seniority. Managing directors and senior general managers, for example, enjoy a considerable degree of discretion in the performance of their jobs and, as such, the parameters within which they operate are rather broadly defined (Kotter, 1982). By contrast, junior managers work within far more narrowly prescribed roles. Even so, most enjoy some degree of choice – certainly by comparison with most other categories of employees – such that they are left to make decisions, take on responsibilities and exercise personal judgement. It is this aspect of their work that can often represent important sources of both job satisfaction and stress since the exercise of discretion requires an ability to cope with ambiguity and operational uncertainty (Cooper and Marshall, 1978b). Thus, if decision-making can be a challenging experience, it can also create anxieties and doubts. This, perhaps, explains why some managers deliberately become preoccupied with routine administrative matters in order to avoid many of the responsibilities and uncertainties often associated with decision-making.

More generally, there is some evidence in Britain and the United States to suggest that there is an increasing polarization of management tasks within large-scale organizations (Child, 1984; Smith, 1988). The adoption of computer-based monitoring systems and the wider use of task-related performance indicators, for example, has in some cases reduced the managerial discretion of many junior and middle-level managers and reinforced the concentration of decision-making among limited numbers of senior managers responsible for longer-term corporate strategy (Buchanan and Boddy, 1983; Carter, 1985). Consequently, those junior managers who are increasingly expected to achieve precisely delineated objectives find that they are subject to even tighter constraints. As a result, they may perceive their jobs to be less psychologically rewarding. At the same time, if staff levels are cut in order to reduce overheads, the remaining managers may be expected to carry existing and, in some cases, greater workloads. Consequently, they find that their perennial complaints of overload are seriously exacerbated by resource cutbacks. This is often reflected in the need to work longer simply in order to meet the minimum expected standards of performance. In our study, for example, 84 per cent of the 323 men and 88 per cent of the 51 women managers claim they work an average week in excess of fifty hours and most state that this has increased significantly over recent years. As we might expect, because of tendencies towards polarization the trend is most pronounced amongst younger, junior managers. Figure 2.1 shows that 67 per cent of younger men and 80 per cent of younger women report an increase in the length of their working week over the past five years.

Many of these younger managers argue that they are overwhelmed with an increasing volume of routine adminis- trative tasks which they are expected to undertake with no additional resources. The fact that there is 'too much to do and too little time' has always been a complaint of managers (Cooper and Marshall, 1978b; French and Caplan, 1973), but the *intensification* of these pressures within their own working lives is particularly evident among those who are younger and in more junior positions.

There's pressure on getting things done. Timetables. Every- thing always seems to be demanded yesterday. I suppose that's the main problem over the last twenty years. Every- thing seems to have got quicker. Answers are required yesterday. That's really what I'm saying. That's one of the main problem areas. (male, late 30s, Finance and Accounting).

We get more and more work to be crammed into the same amount of time. Staff are cut – pared to the bone and quite

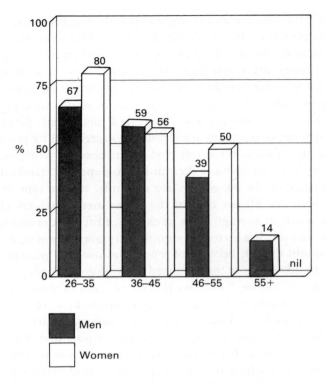

Figure 2.1 Men and women managers in different age groups reporting an increase in length of working week.

often, we are working four, five or six under basic staff . . . Pressures of work are such that you come in early even though we're officially nine to five. You're expected to come in at eight, work through your lunch hour . . . and work late at night as well on occasions . . . It can tell after a while, obviously . . . If you're not prepared to put more than the nine to five in, I don't think you'll get very far . . . In this industry, one is always working to a timescale and work has to be done regardless of whether it's physically possible . . . You have to bring work home in order to fulfil that. I don't bring work home out of any pleasure, purely because I have to. (male, late 20s, Administration).

[24]

The most stress comes from being very tired . . . this is a very commercial company – part of a big, cut-throat group. The sheer hard work! I think I do a 14-hour day most days . . . It's just the environment. It's expected. It eventually builds up and creates a lot of stress. (female, late 20s, Personnel).

Men and women managers, then, are prone to being overburdened with excessive work tasks. Accordingly, their experiences of stress may be caused by this rather than by the need to cope with complex duties or responsibilities. This can, of course, be exacerbated by a reluctance to delegate, even within bureaucratic structures which are deliberately designed to accomplish goals through the systematic delegation and depersonalized allocation of work tasks. Typically, they feel overworked yet underutilized in the sense that their personal talents and skills are not properly developed (Alban-Metcalfe and Nicholson, 1984). Many feel, as a result, that they stand the risk of being regarded as 'ineffective' by their immediate bosses. Indeed, the problems are compounded in many organizations by pressures to cut costs through staff reductions which force those who remain to undertake tasks which are beyond their specialist competences. Thus, as jobs are 'redesigned', 'collapsed' and 'renegotiated', managers are often required to perform duties for which they have neither ability nor inclination. It is unlikely that this kind of 'job enlargement' will lead to them experiencing an increased sense of challenge and psychological fulfilment. Indeed, without appropriate skills or knowledge they are likely to be confused and frustrated, yet few, it seems, have access to training and development programmes which might help them overcome such deficiencies (Handy, 1987). Amongst those in our survey we attempted to gauge the extent to which such conditions might be associated with various physical and psychological symptoms of stress. Of course, generalizations are difficult if only because similar pressures may evoke different responses among different individuals. Some, for example, may be better equipped to cope with

[25]

stress than others, and are likely to suffer fewer detrimental personal consequences (McMichael, 1978). Nevertheless, a range of psychological and behavioural conditions – such as aggression, irritability, frustration and tiredness – are often correlated with 'high-pressure' work environments (Davidson and Cooper, 1983). In our questionnaire we asked managers personally to assess the incidence of these, on a scale ranging from 'never' to 'always'. Of the various items scored, 'frustration', 'fatigue' and 'mental exhaustion' represent the most frequently experienced. As Figure 2.2 shows, almost four in ten men and women report feelings of frustration 'often' or 'always'.[2]

Of course, such responses – alone – can provide only a crude measure of the negative consequences of work. In our in-depth interviews, however, we were able to explore these issues further. Ironically, perhaps, junior and middle-level managers are often frustrated because they feel 'excluded' from *management*. Two men express this view as follows:

Despite the workload . . . I've not been a manager. I've not been able to manage . . . I believe that those above me are unable to function as managers in their sphere. Because it's puppets pulling the strings of other puppets. I can't make an out and out decision on something important without referring – 'Can I do this?' 'Can I do that?'. . . There was a time when I was happy to go to work. There was a time when I would get out of bed in the morning, put my feet on the floor and there was no weariness – no tiredness. Now I put my feet on the floor and think, 'Got to go to work. Got to go to work.' (male, late 40s, Engineering and Maintenance).

The difficult part of my job is the volume. The large number of people I'm dealing with. There's a reorganization going on and it's having its effect on people like me . . . My frustration is mainly with seniors . . . I can't explain why but, quite often, I find these people inadequate . . . When I was appointed, I was told, 'You are now part of the management team.' That was the biggest disappointment of all because you quickly find that you are not. That was the frustration of my

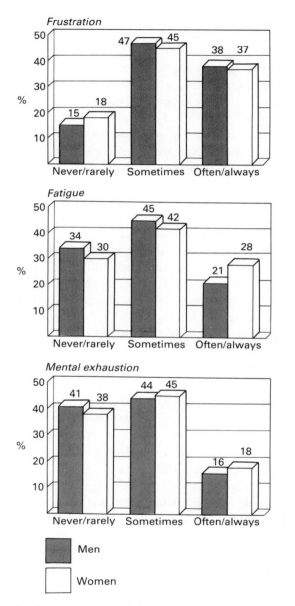

Figure 2.2 The incidence of frustration, fatigue and exhaustion amongst men and women managers.

first managerial job. I didn't get the satisfaction I thought I'd
get out of it. (male, late 20s, Administration).

These experiences suggest a growing divide between, on
the one hand, senior executives and, on the other, middle and
junior managers. The former increasingly appear to mono-
polize strategic decision-making, while the latter are delegated routine administrative duties which are subject to
tighter measures of performance. Those who are unable to
demonstrate their competences through achieving particular
targets can no longer assume, as they may have done in the
past, either security or steady progress into more senior
positions. If, then, promotion can no longer be achieved
primarily on the basis of age, qualification and experience,
they are forced to revise their personal ambitions and life
priorities. For some, this can undermine their adherence to
values which emphasize personal achievement and instead
lead them to develop more 'solidaristic' sentiments. The
growth of unionism among technical, scientific and managerial staff is but one expression of this trend which, in turn,
can exaggerate the tendencies towards greater polarization
within management hierarchies (Bamber, 1976; Gospel,
1978). Perhaps not surprisingly, then, there is evidence that
junior managers are developing common interests with those
who perform routine non-managerial administrative and
service tasks; both groups increasingly recognize that they
constitute an instrumentally exploited and, indeed, expend-
able human resource. They share, as a result, growing
feelings of cynicism as well as a heightened sense of estrange-
ment from the predominant goals and values of their employing organizations. Thus, tighter forms of senior managerial control, together with ongoing processes of rationaliza-
tions and cost reduction, can further undermine their morale
and self-confidence. As three middle managers describe the
process:

> People get despondent. You know for a fact that their heart is
> not in the job. They're not giving you the co-operation . . .

[28]

I've been doing this job for fourteen years now and I know all the guys I've got under me – they're all good guys but their heart is not totally in the job. And, I must say, nor is mine in the way it used to be. With this reorganization hanging over you, you begin to think, 'Oh, for Christ's sake'. . . It's a shame. (male, late 40s, Finance and Accounting).

The economic situation makes people think, 'Well, sod it, you know; what the hell', 'It doesn't matter what I do'. This is particularly noticeable within the manual workforce and at some of the lower clerical levels. There's an attitude that's very hard to correct. You know, 'What the hell does it matter? All I'm interested in is getting as much out of the organization as I can because I've got no long-term future. They can finish me in 13 weeks – that's the extent of my commitment.' And it has had its impact at the middle management level because, to some extent, we're just as much out of control as the others. Although we may be the instruments of the policy and have some input into how the policies are applied, I certainly think, at our level, we can do little to influence the actual policy. If it's decided there will be a reduction of 1,000 jobs, that's the policy. We have to determine how it's done but not what the decision is. (male, early 30s, Personnel).

The reorganization is affecting morale. Morale is very low. Apathy is becoming rampant. And it makes it harder, I consider, for the likes of myself. I regard myself as a very conscientious person but it becomes harder and harder to carry out your tasks and see it gets done properly with the apathy that surrounds you. If you don't beat them you could well end up joining them . . . Speaking for myself, I think I end up joining them. (male, late 40s, Engineering and Maintenance).

As several observers (Barnard, 1938; Drucker, 1974) have pointed out, managers can only achieve their goals through others; they must allocate duties and then monitor their efficient performance. This, of course, assumes that there are well established structural mechanisms which facilitate delegation as well as the availability of competent staff who possess the appropriate aptitudes and skills. But managers often feel that these preconditions are not met, primarily because, in their view, they lack subordinates to whom they feel they can allocate tasks. Some argue that the source of their problems lies in the lack of resources which are devoted to staff training. As several recent surveys show, the majority of managers at all levels in Britain receive little or no formal training other than short-term induction programmes (Handy, 1987; Constable and McCormick, 1987). As such, most are left to acquire their managerial skills through coping with day-to-day problems. The situation is compounded when, through reorganization and cost-cutting exercises, relatively responsible duties are allocated to under-qualified, inexperienced subordinates. In such circumstances, few managers possess the confidence to delegate and, as a result, their own workloads are increased. The views of three managers are typical:

> To be honest, the thing I really find most frustrating is the disappointment that occurs when people of whom you have an expectation of performance fail to live up to it . . . Disappointment in the performance of others is the biggest frustration . . . As a result, I think I am a very selective delegator. (male, early 50s, Finance and Accounting).

> There are certain things I feel I want to stay on top of. I want to be on the ball. But I have to handle it myself because I don't think the staff under me are of sufficient calibre. Things that I delegate to them I just have to do again. (male, early 30s, General Management).

> I think that the job would be wonderful if we didn't have any people . . . That's the hardest thing. To get people to work effectively. A lot of people will work but they don't work effectively . . . I have to resist the temptation of saying, 'Get out of the way, I'll do it myself'. . . It's a big problem when you know full well you can do it better. (male, early 30s, General Management).

[30]

But the problem does not rest solely with their subordin-ates. Some managers recognize that their *own* personal skills are inadequate.[3] In particular, they are often acutely aware of shortcomings in their knowledge of human relationships and in the supervision of other people. Most of them will, of course, have been promoted on the basis of their *technical* competences and personal compatability rather than their expertise in *managerial* skills and yet, in many ways, the supervision and motivation of staff has become particularly demanding during recent years. As a result of corporate cost-cutting exercises and restructuring, there are fewer opportunities for managers to reward their staff with promo-tion and automatic pay increases and, instead, they are subject to greater pressures to extract more effort from a static or declining number of staff (Smith, 1988). One manager sums up the personal impact of these changes as follows.

> The manpower has remained static but the job has grown. So the pressures have got greater because of the cutbacks . . . so it gets sharper. Decisions get that much more difficult to make. The job gets more demanding . . . Judgement is the name of the game. Choices have bigger risks attached to them . . . Whereas once we would have nursed someone who didn't make the grade, now the pressures are greater. In dealing with people, there's not the freedom to be so accom-modating. So, in that sense, the job has got more demanding. (male, early 40s, Computing).

Managers are also experiencing tensions because of the increasing extent to which they are being made accountable for the achievement of performance-related targets. Accord-ingly, they often see themselves as subject to conflicting and often irreconcilable expectations. If the frustrations associated with their own staff can sometimes be resolved, this is less often the case in their relationships with immediate bosses upon whom, of course, they are heavily dependent in terms of promotion prospects and salary increases. When combined with the growing need to achieve measurable results, this can

[31]

constitute the basis for considerable job dissatisfaction. Four
managers describe the pressures in these terms:

> One of the pressures is fear of failure . . . the day of account-
> ability has come . . . Jobs aren't on the line because of one
> mistake, but certainly they are if there's continued failure . . .
> Reporting lines are now much stricter and tighter. If you've
> made a mess up, it comes to light quicker . . . and the
> consequences for being out of line are more immediate and
> severe than perhaps they have been in the past. (male, early
> 30s, Administration).

> We must apply a much more vigorous approach to examining
> the things that we do and the reasons for them. That's
> increased the pressure . . . there's simply less money. The
> days of luxury have gone. We've got to sit down and take
> very difficult decisions . . . It increases the pressure. (male,
> late 20s, Personnel).

> Our employers are putting pressure on. Money must be
> saved. It's not getting easier. You used to be able to get away
> with things . . . now you need a proper justification – a well
> thought out argument. They [senior managers] are far more
> informed now and there's a need for value for money. So your
> head goes on a block a bit more often. That causes you
> concern and leads to stress. (male, late 40s, Computing).

> You may not agree with everything your boss says but you're
> not always in a position to argue with them. So that can be a
> bit frustrating. I think this is something which I experience
> more than I ever did and a lot of my colleagues at my level feel
> the same . . . it's becoming very strained. Staff are expected
> to work much harder than ever before . . . But when they see
> their hard efforts being lost by the stroke of a pen, it's rather
> frustrating and people are beginning to wonder whether it's
> worthwhile slogging their guts out. (male, late 40s, Account-
> ing and Finance).

These observations are consistent with the findings of
several studies which have focused upon subordinate–
superordinate relationships within management hierarchies

(Cooper and Davidson, 1982; Petty and Bruning, 1980).
Most managers, of course, delegate to others and, at the same
time, are accountable for the performance of tasks which are
delegated to them. It is, then, almost inevitable that tensions
will emerge in such relationships. But how are these vented?
Generally, they cannot be easily expressed at work since
overt frustration with immediate bosses is normally regarded
as unacceptable and can jeopardize career prospects. At the
same time, there are role prescriptions which ensure that
managers behave in relatively non-emotional and affectively
neutral ways (Kanter, 1977; Merton, 1964). Usually, therefore, experiences of stress are sublimated within work settings and discharged to other situations. Thus informal
'lunchtime' and 'drinking' groups offer opportunities for
colleagues to analyse, discuss and review the competences of
their immediate bosses. Equally, domestic relationships may
sometimes offer contexts where such feelings can be expressed and other work-related tensions released (Cooper, 1982).
As an experienced manager remarks:

> Most people, when they're at work, behave in a particular
> way. They tend not to show their emotions to the degree that
> they will at home when they're in their own relaxed atmo-
> sphere. At home . . . your family will put up, to a degree,
> with how you are. When you're at work – because you want
> to create the aura of the manager who knows where he's
> going, what he's doing and why he's doing it – you'll *appear*
> more relaxed. But beneath the surface you may be completely
> knotted up. But you do your best to make sure other people
> don't see that. (male, early 50s, Personnel).

Another means of coping with such tensions is to maintain
a degree of cognitive distance between work role and self-
identity (Goffman, 1959). In this way, individuals may
abdicate any attempts to make any significant creative,
psychological or emotional contributions to their jobs. They
simply perform their duties 'adequately' and redirect their
energies to leisure and home-based pursuits. Work is then

[33]

perceived primarily in instrumental terms: as a source of income which can be used for the pursuit of other, more important and meaningful activities. Older managers, in particular, who may be especially disenchanted with their jobs because they are locked into middle-rank positions, often develop personal 'survival' strategies which allow them to 'get by' and to 'stay out of trouble' (Hunt and Collins, 1983). Consequently, the operating performance of many organizations is impaired and the career prospects, motivation and commitment of younger managers may be severely curtailed. It is, then, hardly surprising that companies introduce early retirement and voluntary severance schemes which can help to 'shake out' these older managers in order to facilitate the promotion of younger colleagues. However, these and many other attempts to remove sources of managerial dissatisfaction appear to have met with only limited success (Hunt, 1984).

Some claim that a more fundamental resolution to the overload, tensions and conflicts faced by middle managers may be achieved by the continuing application of microelectronic or 'new' technology (Forester, 1987). But whether information technology will enable them to cope better with the complexities and pressures of their jobs or to be part of a 'rationalization strategy' which actually reinforces or exaggerates the difficulties which they already encounter is a matter for conjecture. According to some observers, the continuous adoption of computer-based information systems and microelectronics may lead to more managers handling machines rather than people (Jarrett, 1982; Scott, 1984). Such a view transforms managers into highly qualified 'technicians' who are at the forefront of trends shaping an emerging post-industrial society. In manufacturing companies, for example, changes in production systems have already been brought about by computer-aided design systems, computer-based stock control and numerically controlled machines; in financial services, electronic transfer systems and automated tellers have been introduced; and in public services, there is growing automation of the office through the use, for example, of electronic mailing and tele-conferences (Child, 1984). According to Francis (1986), these kinds of technological changes are likely to impact on managerial work in at least four major ways:

> One obvious change will be that the first management jobs to be automated will be the very routine tasks. Laborious tasks of checking through figures and searching for data that relate to the control of people or functions under the manager's direction are those most likely to be the first to be put on the manager's personal computer or provided by the automated office system to which he or she has access . . . A second effect is likely to be a reduction in the number of people under the control of any one manager and an increase in the amount of capital equipment. This will be most marked in offices . . . A third factor changing the nature of managerial work, and associated with the introduction of more capital equipment, is that the qualifications of those being supervised by the average manager are likely to increase. With the more routine work automated and with more capital equipment to be operated, the number of unskilled jobs is likely to fall . . . A fourth factor associated with this last factor, is that the work done by these more highly qualified subordinates will be more complex than in the past. (pp.132–3).

These changes will, in turn, place new demands on managers and their organizations:

> The manager now has to operate with a different style of supervision. He or she is likely to shift from a strategy of direct control to a strategy of responsible autonomy. The better qualified subordinates doing more complex tasks which require more judgement, and whose productivity is not tied to the production line, are likely to require more autonomy; there should be higher trust between manager and subordinate; and a participative management style is likely to be more effective. A different organization culture is likely to be more appropriate: one which is less formal, less rule bound, more flexible, and task centred rather than role centred, is likely to be more effective in the new circumstances. (p.134).

[35]

But if these are some of the major trends predicted by some observers, how do they compare with the reactions and experiences of practising managers? Generalizations are difficult because while some are optimistic about the likely outcomes of new electronic-based technological systems, others are decidedly pessimistic. Figure 2.3 summarizes the

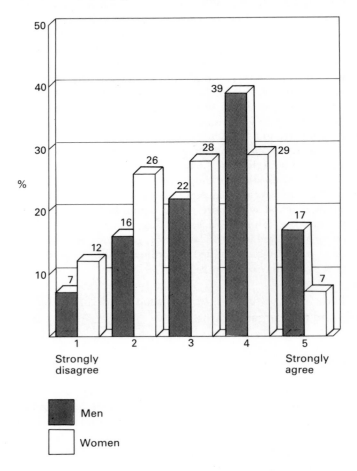

Figure 2.3 How far do you agree or disagree with the claim that 'new technological developments' are increasing the level of stress among managers?

[36]

views of those in our survey concerning the likely impact of technological change on levels of managerial stress.

Some managers – a minority in our survey – are relatively optimistic about the implementation of new technology primarily because they feel it will increase their capacity to handle growing volumes of work and to monitor more closely the behaviour of their colleagues. They argue that it enables them to have direct and rapid access to an increasing amount of complex information while, at the same time, it releases them from some of the more mundane administrative aspects of their work. They feel, then, that they will be more effective as managers because they will have more time for strategic planning, forward thinking and efficient decision-making. Two of them express this view in the following terms:

> New technology is obviously going to improve the information we've got available. We get it quicker and more accurately . . . It will have a big effect on work . . . We have access to more information and, with management training, I think we should make better decisions. Time will be spent less on delving for information because technology makes it available quicker and more accurately . . . It will be more interesting to spend more time actually thinking out a problem rather than digging out the statistics first. (male, late 40s, Computing).

> Managers will be far more able to produce and get information than in the past . . . In the past, managers were very much at the mercy of the people that gave them information – be it the accountants or whatever. The accountant produced the figures and the managers had to make do with them . . . But with small personalized micros, the manager can access more information far quicker and far easier . . . They won't need to ask the accountant . . . Everyone here is now getting more of a computer orientation and it definitely helps. (male, late 40s, Finance and Accounting).

But these views contrast with the argument that technological change will severely de-skill some managers' jobs and, indeed, reduce the need for them. Middle and junior managers, in particular, may feel that these trends are likely to reinforce the polarization of management. Six in ten, by comparison with less than half of the senior managers, feel that technological change will increase stress levels. If, indeed, senior managers can now use new technology for monitoring more closely the performance of their junior colleagues, it seems likely that the opportunities available to the latter for exercising discretion and responsibility will, in turn, be diminished (Smith, 1988). As a result, work could continue to lose many of its intrinsic rewards as present-day management tasks become 'de-skilled', performed by technicians whose primary function is to service computer-based information systems. In our survey, for example, those trained in accounting skills often feel particularly vulnerable. The following comments are illustrative:

> We're in for some quite dramatic changes – particularly in my profession. With new technology, my profession will suffer dramatically. At the moment, there's already a surplus of accountants and a lot of their jobs can be computerized. The new technology will replace a lot of the work we do . . . It doesn't need much to see this. It's all around us. (male, early 40s, Finance and Accounting).

> With new technology accountants will be the first to go . . Certainly, a labour intensive part of society like the public sector is going to be affected by this . . . The accountants that are left are going to have to be 'knowledge engineers'. (male, late 30s, Finance and Accounting).

Of course, as research investigations show, the consequences of technological change are primarily determined by the objectives and strategic priorities of those who are responsible for its introduction and implementation. 'The changes to organizational structure that accompany technological change', say the authors of a series of recent case studies, 'reflect strongly and directly the expectations and objectives of management, and weakly and indirectly the characteristics of the technology' (Buchanan and Boddy, 1983, p.244). Within more competitive and uncertain conditions, the senior managers of large-scale corporations have been primarily concerned to implement 'new' technologies in order to cut overheads, reduce manning levels, tighten performance measures and generally strengthen their command over the whole management process (Child, 1984). However, there are other circumstances when the objectives of senior management are to introduce systems in order to improve quality control and to encourage more adaptive and flexible work practices. Thus, the implementation of 'new' technologies can increase the level of skill required of managers and other technically qualified staff. This can more often be the case in less bureaucratically structured organizations when, because of continuous pressures to be responsive to changing markets, managers often require working autonomy in order to undertake their specialist tasks. In more tightly controlled, centralized structures, on the other hand, computer-based information processes may strengthen the hierarchical control mechanisms which are used to monitor the performance of middle and junior managers (Boddy and Buchanan, 1986).

Although some managers may have strong opinions as to the likely effects of new technology, others feel it is of little importance. This is often because, so far, it has not radically changed the nature of their day–to–day working practices. Indeed, some are keen to distance themselves from its impact: particularly older managers and those who occupy positions in general as distinct from specialist management functions. According to Forester (1987), this kind of indifference has significantly delayed its implementation in many large-scale organizations:

> Too many managers prefer to carry on in the same old way and won't explore new methods of working. They feel threatened by the new technology and fear loss of power to those more familiar with computers. 'Wait and see' conservat-

ism all too often triumphs. In the United Kingdom, a major survey by the Policy Studies Institute in 1983 on progress and problems with the electronic office found the biggest single reason for not investing in new technology was that it had simply never been considered. Many managers lacked the knowledge or commitment to even investigate the possibility of going over to automation. (p.209).

For these managers it is perhaps not surprising that new technologies are little more than an abstraction – something which they read about in technical journals or discuss on management training programmes but about which, in their daily lives, they have only limited experience. Accordingly, their views may have a 'secondhand' flavour, because often they are doing no more than simply reiterating accounts of other people's experiences.[4] Even those who use more advanced computer systems can adhere to work practices which militate against more fundamental changes. One senior manager touches on this theme in the following comments:

> I feel that we've all been conditioned as managers to believe that new technology is affecting the way we work and the way we live. At the moment, I think it's just not true. I find it very interesting speaking to managers. They're still waiting for the revolution. They may have VDUs flickering away in the room next door . . . and they may talk to their screen. But all they're doing is mapping onto screen things that were done manually before. All right, they're faster, but it's not really affecting the way the office is working. We've still got to be hit by the new technology . . . At the moment, we pay lip service to it all. (male, late 30s, Finance and Accounting).

However, despite differences in their opinion about its immediate impact, many managers agree that new technologies *are* important although they are not quite sure of the reasons why. Some are keen to present themselves as enthusiastic because of the associated connotations with 'progress' and 'efficiency'; others are far more cautious because of the possible threats to their jobs. Although the evidence remains inconclusive, it would seem that, on balance, these fears may be well-grounded. As Boddy and Buchanan (1986) observe:

> major computer installations have often set off a radical review of management structures. That, in association with economic pressure, seems to be threatening many middle and junior management positions, especially those associated with routine information processing jobs. (p.158).

While, then, various pundits predict radical transformations in future work practices, there is considerable cynicism and doubt among managers. Certainly, they can feel threatened by present-day developments in office technology since they reinforce their uncertainties and anxieties over the future of their jobs and the restructuring of their employing organizations.

In this context, it is worth asking whether those in management positions still feel they are able to derive a sense of personal satisfaction from their jobs. It may be, given the experiences we have described, that their work preferences have changed. It is possible that large organizations can no longer offer, or even promise, the degree of satisfaction which the majority of them once expected from their jobs and careers. In order to investigate this, we included in our questionnaire a number of measures of job satisfaction of the sort often used by social psychologists.[5] Thus, in our own study we attempted – albeit in a relatively crude fashion – to identify some of the more important rewards that managers expect from their employment. It is often claimed, for example, that they want opportunities for decision-making and for exercising discretion and judgement (Stewart, 1982). Further, it is argued that they prefer to work in relatively unsupervised circumstances where they can enjoy a high measure of autonomy and independence in the performance of their tasks (Herzberg, Mausner and Snyderman, 1959). It is alleged that they seek out jobs which will enable them to obtain a high degree of self-fulfilment through the utilization of their personal talents and skills (Morse and Weiss, 1955).

[41]

However, if such 'intrinsic' rewards are considered to be important so, too, are the various 'extrinsic' benefits, such as level of remuneration, opportunities for promotion, security and personal status which they derive from their jobs (Poole et al., 1981). Clearly, the relative preferences for these different 'intrinsic' and 'extrinsic' rewards will vary considerably according to age, level of seniority, functional or technical specialism and many other factors. It would, for instance, be surprising if the expectations and desired rewards of older and more senior male sales managers were similar to those of younger women in junior personnel functions. Even so, *all* managers are by comparison with most other categories of employees privileged in that they can expect *both* high 'intrinsic' and 'extrinsic' rewards from their jobs.[6] However, in view of the changes we have discussed in this chapter, it is of interest to determine how far traditional expectations are being met. This is particularly so given the extent to which there seems to be a growing polarization between the work experiences of those in more senior positions and others who feel they are subject to tighter controls and increasingly required to undertake a growing volume of routine administrative duties.

We address this issue in different ways at various points throughout this book. Here we do so in a preliminary fashion in terms of the extent to which management jobs offer various intrinsic and extrinsic rewards. Using measures originally developed by Porter (1961) and adapted in a British Institute of Management survey (Mansfield et al., 1981) those in our study were asked to rate their own jobs according to the presence or absence of a variety of factors. As with many conventional measures of managerial satisfaction, these broadly correspond with Maslow's (1954) need hierarchy as follows: security (safety need); self-respect and personal status (ego–esteem need); independent thought and action (ego–autonomy need); personal growth and development (self–actualization need). As with the BIM survey, we also asked managers to rate their pay and promotion prospects.

[42]

Needless to say, any attempt to separate and measure the perceived importance of such factors will inevitably simplify the complexity and the interrelatedness of their nature. It can be argued, for example, that managers' dissatisfaction with promotion opportunities may simply reflect a wish for more pay or a growing frustration with the limited possibilities that their jobs may offer for experiencing a sense of personal growth or self-fulfilment. Equally, the desire to work in relatively unsupervised conditions may be inextricably linked, for some, with feelings of personal esteem or status. However, notwithstanding such limitations, Tables 2.1 and 2.2 do provide some indication of the rewards which managers obtain from their jobs and which they regard as important. More precisely, they show on a seven–point scale ranging from 'low' to 'high', the extent to which managers feel various rewards are *actually* present with the degree to which they *desire* them.

An initial glance at Tables 2.1 and 2.2 suggests that although managers attach considerable importance to opportunities for exercising independent judgement and thought and for developing their personal talents and skills, there is some feeling that their expectations in these terms are not being fulfilled. This is illustrated in the discrepancies between their expectations and what they *actually* enjoy; for 'personal growth' there is a difference of 1.2 for men and 1.0 for women. For 'independent thought', there is a contrast of 0.9 for both men and women. These findings may be linked to the fact that managers are compelled to devote a greater proportion of their time to the execution of routine matters and, in the performance of these, to be subject to tighter forms of higher managerial control. At the same time, they appear to be less than fully satisfied with their salaries and career prospects. The latter, perhaps, is a reflection of their awareness of how organizational changes and the redesign of management jobs may be limiting their chances for longer-term advancement. Indeed, of all the discrepancies between 'actual' and 'desired' job characteristics, that for

[43]

Table 2.1 Sources of Job Rewards as Perceived by Men and Women Managers

Own job offers opportunity for:	Mean Score (1 = low; 7 = high)	
	Men	Women
Self-respect/esteem and status	5.4	5.3
Independent thought and action	5.3	5.1
Security	5.0	4.9
Pay	4.5	4.4
Personal growth	4.4	4.8
Promotion	3.7	3.9

Table 2.2 Desirability of Job Rewards as Perceived by Men and Women Managers

Desirability of:	Mean Score (1 = low; 7 = high)	
	Men	Women
Independent thought and action	6.2	6.0
Security	6.0	5.4
Self-respect/esteem and status	5.9	6.1
Pay	5.6	5.3
Personal growth and development	5.6	5.8
Promotion	5.2	5.3

'promotion' is the most striking (1.5 for men and 1.4 for women).[7]

The relatively high priority attached to 'security' is also of interest and expresses, we suspect, the increasing uncertainties that managers feel about their jobs; they can no longer assume they will be continuously employed and, as a result, tenure has become increasingly valued as an occupational reward. However, there does seem to be a difference between men and women, with the latter being less likely to attach such importance to security. This, of course, may be a result of the greater incidence of career interruption which they experience as a result of family obligations, geographical moves associated with partners' job changes and, sometimes, an assumption among those who are married – that their husbands can financially 'underwrite' any career-related risks (Marshall, 1984).

However, it is important to bear in mind the sharp contrasts in the experiences of both men and women managers which can be concealed within the overall responses. There are differences, for example, among the managers in our study according to such attributes as age, seniority and, indeed, gender. Older and more senior male managers tend to be more satisfied than others. By their late 40s and early 50s, those who see themselves as successful in their careers are normally in positions which confer status, offer relatively high financial rewards and provide possibilities for the full utilization of personal talents and abilities. Other older managers who are, perhaps, less successful, and who are confronted with declining prospects for promotion, tend to readjust their expectations and to adapt psychologically by, for example, developing interests outside work or even by anticipating early retirement. Thus they may 'role play' and, in doing so, minimize their feelings of discontent. By contrast, *younger men* and, to some extent, *older women* are more likely to be dissatisfied with particular aspects of their jobs. These differences are clear from Tables 2.3 and 2.4 which report the total percentage discrepancies between the rewards managers want from their jobs compared with what they obtain, according to age, gender and seniority.

Clearly, there are a number of factors that may account for the dissatisfactions of younger men and older women but many would seem to be associated with their concentration in middle and junior managerial positions. As such, they are less likely to be able to utilize their personal talents and skills fully and to be in positions whereby they can exercise discretion and judgement in relatively underutilized circumstances. Indeed, one in four feel their skills are underscrutinized by comparison with one in ten senior managers. Many of them are obliged to undertake routine administrative tasks and feel

[45]

Table 2.3 Job Dissatisfaction – Age and Gender (Percentage Differences in Actual and Desired Job Rewards)

Job Rewards	Men			Women		
	25–34	35–44	45–54	25–34	35–44	45–54
Opportunities for personal growth	24	15	12	14	10	22
Opportunities for independent thought	14	13	13	15	7	19
Security	12	16	15	3	14	18
Pay	14	15	15	14	8	19
Promotion	30	22	20	22	16	26
Esteem/status	10	7	4	14	10	6

that their future career prospects are highly limited. In addition, younger women are often restricted in their career opportunities because of predominant male assumptions about their suitability for appointment to senior positions. It is, then, hardly surprising that they, in particular, are likely to be more dissatisfied than their male colleagues. Indeed, if a more detailed analysis is undertaken of the nature of their particular sources of discontent, it is evident that these are in terms of 'promotion' and the opportunities available for 'personal growth'. Younger men who share these dissatisfactions can, by contrast, reasonably hope to be promoted out of the more routine managerial tasks. Even so, the work experiences of both groups may reflect the increasing polarization which is occurring within some management struc-

Table 2.4 Job Dissatisfaction According to Seniority (Percentage differences in Actual and Desired Job Rewards[a])

Job Rewards	Senior	Middle	Junior
Opportunities for personal growth	10	19	18
Opportunities for independent thought	7	13	14
Security	11	13	14
Pay	6	18	20
Promotion	17	24	25
Esteem/status	4	4	12

[a] The insufficient number of women in senior managerial positions in our study prevents us from incorporating the effects of gender in this analysis.

tures. As decision-making become increasingly concentrated within senior positions, junior and middle managers feel they obtain fewer 'intrinsic' rewards. They find their jobs less challenging as their tasks are more closely monitored according to precisely determined targets. Accordingly, they may become preoccupied with short-term objectives and, as such, feel they are given only limited opportunities for exercising their personal talents and skills. Such feelings are strongly expressed as the following comments illustrate:

> At my level, we've got a number of targets to meet . . . we have weekly and monthly targets . . . the financial targets pressure you. You can be totally convinced you're doing a

wonderful job . . . you're getting everything together at the right times, but it doesn't last long . . . Everyone says 'Great' on the Friday. We tot all the figures up at 5 o'clock and say 'Great'. But you come in on Monday and that's gone. Now that's the high point. You've done what was expected, but, on Monday, you're back in and you've got nothing. There's another million pounds to find and you've got the same problems all over again. The successes are very short-lived because you can't dwell on yesterday. You've got to be active today. You've got to look to tomorrow and you've got to keep going . . . The highs are very short-lived and you've got so many targets all the time. (male, late 30s, Production).

There's a lot of pressure to get targets – number of accounts, amount of lending, credit money. There's a lot of pressure on you to look at those figures every month. Every quarter you get print-outs and then you have to advise why, if you can't get within 5 per cent of the target . . . it can be devastating . . . You sell a large amount of insurance one year and the next year your target is increased accordingly, no allowances made. The system is unreal. (male, late 40s, Finance and Accounting).

The management approach is one that engenders fear. The firm has become decreasingly personal and it tends to rule in a harder, more commercial way. To an extent, that's understandable . . . But the bottom line seems to count for everything. The attitude seems to be, 'We don't care how the hell we get on with it as long as we get on with it.' But it has brought with it certain problems. I think that working relationships are more aggressive . . . people are very anxious to look after number one and be seen to do the right thing. A lot of people's time seems to be spent looking over their shoulder to make sure they keep everything clean. It's a sense of self-survival. (male, early 40s, Finance and Accounting).

If, then, managers – particularly those in middle and junior positions – are experiencing sources of dissatisfaction in their jobs, how far are these being compensated by more 'extrinsic' financial rewards? The answer, as suggested in Tables 2.1 and 2.2, would seem to be only to a limited extent. There is a relatively high discrepancy between what they actually receive in terms of their pay compared with what they want. In fact, in our survey, 54 per cent of the men and 43 per cent of the women feel inadequately rewarded and, of these, 63 per cent of the former and 78 per cent of the latter consider they would need increases of at least £2,000 per annum. This is, perhaps, surprising since managers have enjoyed relatively generous pay increases and tax reductions throughout the 1980s. Indeed, in the year prior to our survey managerial salaries increased by about 5 per cent in real terms; approximately twice that gained, for example, by manual workers (British Institute of Management, 1985). This brought average annual salary levels nationally to between about £12,000 and £14,000 for men and £8,000 and £10,000 for women (Department of Employment New Earnings Survey, 1985). Earnings of senior managers were considerably higher, averaging from £19,000 to around £27,000 (British Institute of Management, 1985). In our own study, 75 per cent of the men and 90 per cent of the women earn between £10,000 and £20,000 per annum. But then, of course, these earnings are enhanced by various fringe benefits. The widespread use of these as part of their reward packages is illustrated in Figure 2.4.

Why, then, are they dissatisfied with their financial rewards? There are several factors that need to be taken into account. First, salary increases must be set within the context of changing job demands. Thus, any salary improvements may be regarded as inadequate if they are not seen as sufficient to compensate for undertaking more demanding and stressful job tasks. Further, the increases enjoyed by *most* managers have been outstripped by those of senior corporate executives, who have obtained particularly large increases through peformance-related, bonus schemes (Regional Rewards Surveys, 1985). Indeed, this widening salary gap is reflecting and, in turn, reinforcing the process of polarization to which we have referred. At the same time, many continue to feel deprived by virtue of the comparisons which they

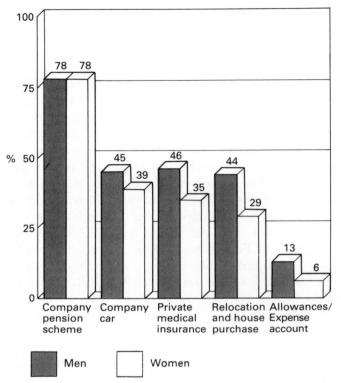

Figure 2.4 Men and women managers receiving various 'fringe' benefits.

make with *other* occupational groups. Hence, in our study, 70 per cent are of the opinion that it is groups of independent professionals – solicitors, accountants, consultants and so on – who have benefited most in financial terms over recent years. Such comparisons are significant because they highlight the dissatisfactions which they experience. As such, the professions are seen to enjoy a variety of rewards which they, as managers, feel they are less likely to experience in their jobs; that is, opportunities for the development of their personal talents and skills within relatively self-regulating work settings. Unlike themselves, they feel professionals do not experience restricted promotion opportunities and con-

[50]

tinuous appraisal and assessment. They are seen to enjoy considerable extrinsic and intrinsic rewards and to be relatively free from the constraints of corporate structures and senior managerial control systems. Indeed, even in the early 1970s, the Pahls (1971) noted that managers admire and envy the male professional because he is seen as

> Someone who could hold his own against the system. His skill would be his capital and this could not be devalued. He would not be obliged to move about. It is similarly assumed that he would not be obliged to work long hours but would have the ideal 'balance': a high status and respected position, 'enough' money and more autonomy in making his important life-plan decisions. (p.262).

Irrespective of the precise accuracy of such images, they do confirm the feelings of disenchantment which are becoming increasingly apparent among managers; particularly among those in middle-level and junior positions whose job experiences are rapidly changing. If, in the past, they may have exchanged a relatively high level of organizational commitment for security of employment and reasonably predictable increases in status and pay, many now find that senior managers are less able or willing to offer such rewards. Increasing operational uncertainties, together with greater pressures to reduce costs, mean that these traditional rewards are less available. Instead, middle and junior managers are compelled to perform increasingly routine tasks and to achieve goals with limited resources and, often, inadequate training. Many feel 'overworked' and yet 'underutilized' in the sense that their jobs offer them only limited opportunities for developing personal talents and skills. Accordingly, as management systems become increasingly polarized between those in senior positions of responsibility and those who are condemned to executing routine tasks in highly controlled work settings, the latter are more inclined to reappraise the priority of work in their lives. How, then, are these emergent problems of motivation amongst middle and junior managers

[51]

being tackled? In the next chapter we assess the extent to which strategies based upon organizational restructuring and appeals to corporate ideals are able to overcome feelings of dissatisfaction as these are associated with the 'close' monitoring of work tasks, and the underutilization of personal skills.

Notes

1 It is generally accepted that developments in technology and the application of the principles of scientific management have largely de-skilled many white-collar and manual occupations. For a 'classical' discussion see Braverman (1974).
2 We are aware of the ambiguous and imprecise nature of stress which clearly has implications for its analysis and measurement. Here, we have chosen to adhere to those indices conventionally used in occupational psychology. See, for example, Davidson and Cooper (1983).
3 As we discuss in Chapter 3, a large proportion of managers recognize their need for further training in this area. Indeed, there has been a significant increase in the demand for 'interpersonal skills' training over recent years from large-scale organizations.
4 During our in-depth interviews, for example, it was evident while discussing 'new' or 'information' technology that respondents were often unable to draw upon first-hand experience of its use.
5 Again, as with our analysis of stress, we used a number of conventional measures, although fully aware of their operational limitations. As such, we regard these as little more than crude indicators of sources of job satisfaction and dissatisfaction.
6 Certainly, by comparison with many routine white-collar and industrial manual workers whose job tasks usually offer little in the form of intrinsic rewards.
7 This finding is consistent with that of the most recent survey conducted by the British Institute of Management (Alban-Metcalfe and Nicholson, 1984).

CHAPTER 3

Organizational change and management style

In the previous chapter, we discussed the changing nature of managers' jobs and how these are affecting their expectations from work. However, it is self-evident that managerial work is essentially a social activity and, as such, that managers' duties and responsibilities can only be understood within the context of specific organizational settings. Hence, any attempt to 'isolate' job tasks in order to measure or compare individual performance in contrasting organizations is likely to be thwarted because of the difficulties of separating these from the contexts within which they are structured.[1] Most managers work within networks of social relationships – which may or may not be prescribed by 'formal' rules and regulations – and consist of superordinates, subordinates, colleagues within and across various departments, divisions and operating units, and various others working both within and outside their own employing organizations. Thus, an essential dimension of management is to create and sustain systems of authority and patterns of responsibility. Equally, managers' own roles and job duties must be defined according to such structures. Organizations, then, constantly change as a result of the interactions of their participating actors.[2] An important task for managers, and particularly for those in senior positions, is to maintain and to modify operating structures so that they are appropriate for accomplishing various goals. At the same time, it is important to recognize that in addition to having formally prescribed structures, organizations operate by reference to a variety of values and assumptions which can be equally as important for

[53]

shaping patterns of behaviour, modes of interaction and the achievement of goals (Schein, 1985). These can be particularly significant in determining 'how things get done' as well as for sustaining employee motivation and morale. Thus, one of the major tasks of senior management is not only to establish and maintain effective operating *structures,* but also to determine 'standards' and 'values' which also regulate behaviour (Peters and Waterman, 1982). It is, then, hardly surprising that organizational structures and their so-called 'cultures' are usually closely interrelated. If the former consist of rules and procedures determining the nature of job duties and work roles, the latter are important for establishing *how* these are performed and interpreted.[3]

In Chapter 1, we suggested that models of effective management based upon the classical bureaucratic model are being queried by those which emphasize the desirability of 'looser', 'flatter' and more 'decentralized' organizational forms (Kanter, 1983; Morgan, 1986). We argued that there are a number of forces underlying such trends, including the need to cut costs by reducing various managerial and supervisory functions; the desire to create more adaptive and responsive operating units; and the need to measure and monitor more closely the output and performance of middle and junior managers. A further objective of such strategies is to abolish organizational attributes which foster among managers risk-averse and non-creative forms of behaviour. Much of the popularity of the bureaucratic paradigm rests upon the degree to which organizational structures, characterized by the clear delineation of work tasks and responsibilities, sustain relatively reliable, predictable and compliant patterns of behaviour (Burns and Stalker, 1961; Gouldner, 1954; Weber, 1947; Woodward, 1958). Accordingly, it is assumed that goals can be achieved in a planned and orderly manner and with a minimum degree of operating ambiguity. However, there is an increasing recognition of the costs of such structures in terms of their tendency to mould a predominant 'personality type' among staff which values conformity and security (Handy, 1985). Thus, 'reliable', and 'satisfactory' performance are seen as desirable attributes with the result that adaptive and more innovative forms of behaviour are devalued. It is, then, hardly surprising that bureaucratically structured organizations are regarded as more effective in relatively stable markets (Mintzberg, 1979). However, in more dynamic circumstances where client demands are more variable and where there are competing providers, such structures can be less appropriate. As a result, senior managers in many private sector corporations are becoming increasingly interested in developing more entrepreneurial, risk-taking forms of behaviour among their junior colleagues (Minkes, 1987). *Intrepreneurship* is often used to describe the attributes of those managers who, working within 'looser', less clearly-defined structures, adopt many of the attitudes and behaviour supposedly characteristic of 'classical' entrepreneurs (Macrae, 1982; Pinchot, 1985).

There is, then, an increasingly popular organizational model which is based upon principles and assumptions which are in sharp contrast to those underlying more bureaucratically organized structures. Instead of an emphasis upon clearly defined tasks, it is claimed that work roles should be broadly defined according to the need to accomplish *specific* objectives (Mintzberg, 1973). Channels of communication should be 'open' and 'informal' rather than, as in bureaucratic structures, strictly defined by formally prescribed roles of authority. If, then, reliability and conformity are valued attributes in bureaucracies, in more loosely structured organizations, a greater emphasis should be placed upon individuals to be creative in their working practices and to be capable of coping with change and uncertainty. Accordingly, they should be committed to organizational goals and, as such, to be psychologically immersed in their jobs (Pascale and Athos, 1982).

These elements are found in many of the present-day panaceas that are advocated as prescriptions for improving organizational effectiveness. Indeed, they seem to be obtaining growing popularity among senior managers as witnessed,

[55]

for instance, in the worldwide success of Peters and Water-man's *In Search of Excellence* (1982). In this book, the authors suggest that highly profitable companies have been able to reduce their reliance upon highly formalized structures and to implement practices which encourage, among other things: 'a bias for action'; 'autonomy and entrepreneurship'; 'produc-tivity through people'; 'hands on, value driven' leadership; and 'simultaneously loose–tight' organizational properties. Similarly, other advocates of organizational change stress the desirability of 'simple structures', 'adhocracies' (Mintzberg, 1979) and 'matrices' (Kolodny, 1981). Hence, it is argued that small and medium-sized companies enjoy considerable competitive advantages because their chief executives, who are often owner managers, are able to exercise direct and simple control over their employees through cultivating open and informal communication systems (Scase and Goffee, 1987). Similarly, in large-scale organizations it is claimed that the nurturing of 'matrices' and 'adhocracies', typically involving the utilization of ever-changing project teams, represent means for overcoming more rigid depart-mental or functional divisions in order to accomplish particu-lar goals. Further, in some large organizations, the need for greater responsiveness to changing markets is reflected in shifts towards 'decentralization' (Morgan, 1986). Companies which are divisionalized on the basis of markets and products are attempting to reinforce the relative autonomy of these units through devolving systems of budgetary control and by introducing various performance-related monitoring schemes. Some have even gone so far as to abandon altogether their divisionalized structures and to substitute in their place wholly-owned subsidiary companies. These can enjoy almost total operating independence for the purposes of generating satisfactory returns on capital employed according to levels determined by their parent holding companies. Consistent with this, and with attempts to 'de-bureaucratize' operating processes, greater efforts are being devoted to training staff in ways which encourage their psychological immersion in the practices, aims and purposes of their organizations (Pascale, 1985). In many companies, this is regarded as the most suitable response to the problems of declining motivation, commitment and morale among many of their middle and junior managers (Roskin, 1986).

But just as organizations vary in terms of their structural characteristics so, too, do they differ in the nature of their predominant values and assumptions. Highly bureaucratized organizations, for example, tend to foster role cultures which emphasize the desirability of clearly defined rules and procedures for operating efficiency (Harrison, 1972). These often encourage the adoption of routinized behaviour and, accordingly, lead to a resistance to innovation and change. Established operating procedures will usually be assumed to be both necessary and efficient and as such, not be regarded as cumbersome 'red tape'. Role cultures also tend to sustain values which give priority to 'security' and 'promotion' as suitable rewards for staff who offer, in return, their loyalty and compliance. Within such organizations, therefore, predominant structures and cultures tend to be mutually reinforcing in that employees become moulded into 'bureaucratic personalities' (Merton, 1964). Hence, they develop cognitive styles which reduce their propensity to take risks and generally to develop more innovative practices. It is in response to this that senior managers in many large-scale organizations are attempting to introduce predominant ideals which emphasize the desirability of experimentation, innovation and flexibility. Hence, they are trying to foster values which emphasize goal achievement rather than a rigid adherence to routines and procedures. According to the specification of particular objectives, a high value is attached to innovation and, as such, informal but intensive patterns of consultation and communication among colleagues is encouraged. This often leads to a constant restructuring of work tasks and the regrouping of staff for the purposes of achieving different pre-set goals. Indeed, the importance of direct hierarchical control is underplayed and, instead, task-related ideals en-

[57]

courage the allocation of rewards according to precise measures of performance.[4]

It is not surprising that organizational models which emphasize the desirability of such attributes should be becoming increasingly popular among senior managers. They are seen to offer cost savings because they allow the abolition of some tiers of middle-level staff (Kanter, 1983). But perhaps most importantly, they provide senior managers with a strategy for coping with the declining motivation of some junior and middle managers (Roskin, 1986). However, the implementation of such practices can create tensions in many public sector organizations since, because of their public accountability, they are especially constrained by formalized procedures that are subject to external scrutiny. Thus, in such contexts, the introduction of more task-oriented styles of management can cause considerable confusion and resistance. The subsequent breakdown in operating practices can lead some senior managers – previously 'converted' to the need for looser organizational forms – to actually reassert traditional bureaucratic values and to tighten their controls over operating procedures.[5]

Senior managers in private sector organizations, by contrast, are less constrained by public scrutiny while, at the same time, they are forced to be cost effective, competitive and to provide a return on capital employed. Accordingly, they can respond to the problems of managerial control through adopting more drastic measures. However, despite the attractiveness of adopting various 'non-bureaucratic' procedures there can be counter-productive effects. Although, 'looser' organizational forms may motivate some employees through inducements associated with different performance-related reward schemes, the continuous resetting of targets can destroy important sources of job satisfaction. As we discussed in the previous chapter, many middle and junior managers can experience feelings of frustration because they feel they are subject to even closer forms of personal scrutiny through the on-going use of prenegotiated targets. At the same time, their predisposition to innovate and to take risks can be severely curtailed by insecurities which they feel about the adequacy of their job performance. As a result, attempts by senior managers to encourage more adaptive, flexible working practices may, instead, foster caution and risk-avoidance and, as such, fail to produce any anticipated improvements in output and productivity.

On the face of it, the introduction of task-oriented ideals can reduce the need for organizational rules, particularly if senior managers are able to generate a strong commitment to clearly-stated goals and to create *high trust* relationships (Pascale and Athos, 1982). Fewer managerial and supervisory staff are then required and the associated reduction in costs can give trading advantages in higly competitive markets. However, this is often difficult to achieve except, perhaps, in smaller, owner-controlled enterprises (Scase and Goffee, 1982). In large, multi-product, highly divisionalized organizations managers may often agree over little more than the most vaguely defined corporate objectives and, almost certainly, there will be continuing disputes about the appropriateness of various strategies for achieving them (Johnson and Scholes, 1984). Even so, it is precisely because of such inherent sources of tension, together with the declining job satisfaction of their middle- and junior-level colleagues, that senior managers are attaching so much importance to the expression of visible, well-defined corporate ideals.

Clearly, programmes of organizational restructuring have important ramifications for the ways in which senior managers control their staff. In highly bureaucratized settings, they can rely more upon rules and formally prescribed procedures whereas in looser structures there are fewer explicit guidelines that govern behaviour. Thus, in the relative absence of clearly defined rules and regulations, a greater emphasis has to be placed upon the use of *interpersonal* skills in order to 'encourage' staff to achieve their targets (Hunt, 1986). This is often a source of considerable anxiety for them since it may be incongruent with their past experiences and training. But in the absence of rules as instruments of control, they have little option but to develop these more personal and informal strategies. However, irrespective of senior managers' preference for any particular type of organizational model, most of their middle- and junior-level colleagues respond to their own anxieties by pragmatically cultivating strategies which they perceive to be the most appropriate for their own specific work settings. Hence, it is usually the talents and skills of their immediate colleagues and subordinates which shape their adoption of particular management styles (Bryman, 1986). Certainly, this was emphasized by the managers we interviewed, as illustrated in the following comments:

> I used to work in technical and research type work, putting in management information systems. It was very technical and not really concerned with people. Obviously, you had to argue sometimes with data processing managers about what you wanted . . . Obviously, one is aware of the works of people like McGregor and Theory Y and Theory X, the two types of managers . . . Each manager has his own individual style and, of course, this is changing all the time. A good manager should change his style depending upon the workforce that he has and the tasks to be performed. The management style that I now try to adopt is very much of concern for people that I'm working with – that is, subordinates. I try very much to get involved with them as individuals . . . The benefits are, in my opinion, that people feel that somebody is concerned about them as an individual and that there is also somebody who is prepared to listen to them, and can make things happen for them in the organization . . . They're far more motivated and, at this level, it's crucial. (male, late 30s, Finance and Accounting.)

> My staff are highly skilled. They're different from the clerical and manual workforce. You could not adopt an autocratic style with my people. They wouldn't work it, anyway. They have to be 'carried along'. They have to be 'explained to'. I'm surrounded by people that I've handpicked over the years – they've all been with me a long time . . . Dealing with people who are creative and above average intelligence is, in my

[60]

view, a lot easier than manual workers . . . there it's got to be leadership of a directive type . . . By contrast, I try to tell my people what the job is and leave them to get on with it . . . I try to engender in them self-dedication and drive . . . I delegate as much as I can as part of the process of keeping people involved . . . You have to push it down as far as it can go. There's no other way of doing it. (male, late 20s, Production).

Ways of managing here hit a new stage within the last few years. The idea of the bowler-hatted manager who goes around demanding things and banging his fists has gone away totally. It doesn't work any more. People's attitudes have changed a lot. They won't tolerate that kind of behaviour now. There's more of a psychological approach needed. You need to convince people – talk people into doing things. They want to know *why* they should do it . . . I think involvement in the way the company is run will increase – particularly in a company like this. I've been working here for twelve years now and I'm firmly embedded in the way this firm works. (male, late 40s, Personnel).

These managers, then, responsible for skilled, technical and highly qualified staff, recognize the need to extend some working autonomy to their subordinates in the performance of their tasks so that they can effectively achieve their prenegotiated goals. As such, they often develop 'project teams' and 'task forces', consisting of people who not only possess particular specialist and technical skills but also who are compatible in their 'personalities' and their personal styles (Belbin, 1981). Since these teams often have to be recomposed according to the changing needs of different objectives, managers have to be well-informed in their understanding of human relations. On the one hand, they have to work *with* their subordinates in achieving goals while, on the other, it is necessary for them to give their junior colleagues opportunities for personal discretion. As a result, they are inclined to develop managerial strategies whereby task-related problems are discussed as part-and-parcel of 'shared' decision-making

[61]

processes. It is in such ways that they motivate their staff rather than through more *explicit* forms of managerial control. Indeed, attempts to exercise 'tighter' or 'closer' forms of supervision would be likely to lead to staff resentment, low morale and poor performance (Fielder and Chemers, 1974). It is, then, within those organizations characterized by complex technologies and where there are high skill levels that senior managers are most inclined to avoid the more formalized attributes of bureaucratic settings.

It is for these reasons that managers are now more concerned with the nature and quality of their interpersonal skills and the extent to which they possess the necessary attributes for exercising effective 'leadership'. However, they are often sceptical as to how far these can be acquired through management training programmes. On the contrary, they tend to regard 'leadership qualities' as *personal attributes* which are essentially 'intangible' and independent of particular organizational settings. As a senior manager stated:

> There are skills that can be taught in terms of man management, in terms of handling people . . . There are techniques about handling people who've got various problems, about getting your own way, motivating others. All these things can be taught. But I still believe a lot of it is down to personality – the personality of the guy and how he manages his team . . . You can't make a good manager out of a bad manager if he hasn't got the right personality. You could take him away for a year and he would never come back as a good manager. I have met people on courses that will never manage as long as they live. (male, early 40s, Production).

Indeed, the generally mythical nature of managers' descriptions is confirmed by the variety of personal characteristics to which they refer. While some emphasize the need for 'astuteness', 'imagination' and 'intelligence', others stress the desirability of 'self-confidence', 'forcefulness' and 'integrity'. On the basis of our in-depth interviews, we could produce a lengthy catalogue of the qualities perceived to be necessary

[62]

for effective leadership, the overwhelming majority of which managers find almost impossible to quantify or precisely define. Of course, it could be that it is the very possession of such *non-definable* attributes which enables some managers to be considered by their subordinates and colleagues to be effective leaders. In other words, it is those managers who are perceived to have extraordinary 'charismatic' personal qualities of one kind or another, both within their immediate work and in broader organizational settings, who are usually considered as the effective 'leaders'.

Although managers in more bureaucratically structured organizations do have doubts about their leadership skills, their anxieties can be less evident. A greater emphasis upon *conformity* tends to inhibit the degree to which even the most charismatic managers can impose their own particular leadership styles (Merton, 1964). Instead, they are often able to perform their tasks with only a limited degree of psychological investment. Unlike their colleagues in less-structured organizations they can, through the use of rules and procedures, psychologically distance themselves from their jobs.[6] Indeed, it is for this reason that many are attracted to management in these more bureaucratic settings. The tendencies encouraging conformity are well illustrated in the following comments taken from our in-depth interviews:

Manager: Managers don't necessarily do what they think they should. They do what they think they ought to do. What will please the organization . . . I would like to see organizations allow people to be themselves a little more . . . I've worked for this organization for twenty-three years and I've been conditioned to its style of thinking and doing. And know their requirements. I know what I should and shouldn't do . . . Inevitably, it has had a very big influence on my general way of life.
Partner: I suppose it has taught you discipline. Every now and again you feel you really want to be your own person, don't you? You flare up – to hell with the system, I'm doing it my way. But I'd say 95 per cent of the time you conform to the company's way of doing things.

[63]

Manager: The company likes stereotypes – that's fair comment. I feel that I sometimes sit in meetings and look around and think, 'Bloody hell. I'm one of that lot here!' (male, early 40s, General Management).

'Diplomacy' is something which the organization likes and conformity is an essential ingredient in career progression. This is the downfall, really. We should not be persuaded to conform all the time. We must question and disagree with things . . . But you've got to toe the party line. You've got to say the right things at the right time . . . Looking back over the past twenty years, has it all been worthwhile? The answer is, I've got a nice house, a reasonable standard of living . . . I have a family, I'm tied to the business. I earn a decent salary so that compensates for a lot of things. (male, early 40s, General Management).

Thus, the organizational constraints encouraging personal conformity are, by definition, greater within bureaucratic structures and, as such, personal management styles are more likely to adhere to codes and practices which are imposed and sanctioned by senior managers. Failure to adapt to these can often be interpreted as evidence of low organizational commitment and indicative of failings in reliability and trustworthiness. Consequently, those who do not adhere to prevailing values, as defined by their senior managers, will seriously jeopardize their own career prospects, irrespective of how efficiently and diligently they perform their tasks. Accordingly, there are strong pressures sustaining personal conformity which reinforce the bureaucratic characteristics of many organizations. It is for such reasons that attempts to increase efficiency through the adoption of looser organizational forms often require the appointment of *outsiders* to senior management positions.[7] It is only in this way that new patterns of leadership, management and supervision can be implemented.

In reflecting the essentially hierarchical nature of bureaucratic organizations, there is often a tendency for senior managers to stress the desirability of 'firm' super-

[64]

vision. Accordingly, managerial styles based upon decision-making in consultation with subordinates may be regarded as ineffective and 'weak'. As such, 'team mangement' is often less pronounced and managers are more likely to be required to make decisions *individually* but always, of course, within strictly-defined spheres of responsibility. One of the managers explained his skills in the following terms:

> As far as staff are concerned, I think that you have to be positive. You need to give the appearance of knowing what you're doing because I think staff like nothing less than to be with someone who dithers; who can't make decisions. You must be able to be positive and decisive. That's the biggest requirement for any manager, because staff will take advantage of you if you can't or won't make a decision. (male, late 30s, General Management).

Management styles, then, are usually the outcome of a variety of influences including prevailing organizational values as well as the contingent circumstances of immediate work settings. The interplay of such factors is also shaped by broader socio-economic and political forces. Hence, higher levels of unemployment, limited job opportunities and 'weakened' trade unionism are encouraging managers to view personally assertive styles as more desirable (Salaman, 1989). Developments in the nature of political debate in Britain during the 1980s have encouraged employers and corporate leaders to 'regain' and exercise 'the right to manage'. Although in many organizations this offers a model for the development of appropriate leadership styles, it can create dilemmas for those managers responsible for highly skilled staff who expect a considerable degree of working autonomy. The impact of wider political influences is reflected in the following observations:

> Without wishing to be political, I think the effect of Margaret Thatcher and her style of government has made us, in this company, less sensitive to people – more ready to take the tougher line. That, to a degree, is a good thing because

[65]

management should have the initiative to manage. But there's a danger that this could become an unfettered approach. We could get back to the situation where an employee is just a means of production. We want him from eight in the morning till five at night and for the rest, we're not concerned. (male, late 40s, Production).

I think Maggie's at the back of it all, basically – be that right or wrong. Managers, executives – call them what you like – the people that count, the people that make the decisions, have jumped on Maggie's back to a very large degree. They've seen what she's done with the miners and quite a few other trade unions and so on and I believe they've literally jumped on her back. They're trying to screw people down for all they're worth, you know . . . 'You do what you're asked to do. You do it – no questions asked'! (male, late 40s, Engineering and Production).

It is among *senior* managers that the desirability of personal assertiveness is most frequently pronounced; they stress the need for goals to be achieved through *firm* leadership. This can have *real* consequences for the career experiences of many middle and junior managers since it is, of course, those in senior positions who set the criteria used for assessing individual performance. It is they who determine the career routes of their subordinates and, therefore, in order to be promoted within particular organizational settings, it is generally necessary for younger and more junior colleagues to develop the 'appropriate' leadership skills. As such, 'personal compatibility' as well as performance is an important determinant of career success.

It is for these reasons that some organizations, particularly those which are highly bureaucratized, are characterized by predominant and clearly defined styles of management. Criteria for staff selection and promotion reinforce these as well as the factors according to which managerial effectiveness is assessed. In terms of present-day models, those who are not seen as sufficiently 'assertive' may fail to be promoted beyond middle managerial rank and, as such, they are forced to complement the more highly admired styles of those in more senior positions. Thus, the efficient execution of job tasks and the possession of various technical and professional qualifications are, in themselves, insufficient for obtaining promotion. This can often be a source of considerable frustration as more ambitious and highly qualified younger managers realize that, in sharp contrast to their earlier educational experiences, personal success is determined by patronage and sponsorship as well as by satisfactory perform- ance and goal achievement (Jay, 1967; Kanter, 1977). The inability of younger managers to develop the required inter- personal skills or, alternatively, their refusal to adopt them, can heighten levels of job dissatisfaction and reduce their organizational commitment.

If younger men are faced with such problems these may be particularly acute for women, the majority of whom are employed in male-controlled organizations where gender can be a significant factor in determining suitability for promo- tion (Marshall, 1984). Accordingly, their career success is heavily dependent upon the sponsorship of senior male colleagues (Cooper and Davidson, 1982). Those who refuse to accept this will often jeopardize their prospects while those who do accept 'the rules of the game' are likely to experience personal stress as they attempt to cultivate personal identities which are acceptable to their male colleagues (Goffee and Scase, 1985). Of course, there are contrasting experiences and, in a very limited number of cases, women have been able to achieve positions of senior responsibility as in, for example, some areas of the public sector (Alban–Metcalfe and Nicholson, 1984). In such circumstances, it may be possible for them to shape the preferred styles of management and, as such, what are regarded as desirable personal attributes. However, the significance of gender may be less pronounced in those organizations where the majority of staff are highly skilled and possess advanced educational qualifications. In 'high technology' and 'creative' companies in which gradu- ates constitute a higher proportion of managers, then, gender

[67]

may be less salient than in, for example, traditional manufacturing organizations where management consists overwhelmingly of men with few technical or professional qualifications.[8]

However, irrespective of gender and level of bureaucratization, most managers have anxieties about their ability to motivate and supervise their staff. As such, they are becoming more aware of the *human,* as distinct from the *technical,* aspect of their jobs, and it is within this area they often feel that they need further training. When in our study managers were asked 'What do you think should be the major inputs in management training?', no fewer than 69 per cent of the men and 82 per cent of the women referred to the need for 'human relations' skills such as 'assertiveness', 'team-building' and 'leadership'. By contrast, the need for training in 'technical', 'financial' and 'corporate planning/decision-making' was mentioned by far fewer of them (Figure 3.1).

The concern of both men and women about the nature of their interpersonal skills reflects, to some extent, the confusion which results from competing managerial and organizational paradigms. At the same time, it is also an outcome of their personal career experiences. Most managers have been promoted into their present positions on the basis of their possession of various technical, functional and specialist knowledge and their compatibility with senior colleagues. As such, they have undergone little formal *management* training (Constable and McCormick, 1987; Handy, 1987); instead, they have acquired the necessary skills informally, through observation, on-the-job experience, and a process of 'trial and error'. Such *ad hoc* learning experiences do little to reduce their anxieties about the quality of their interpersonal management abilities. Certainly, they are often confused as to whether the present fashion for personal assertiveness is always the most useful method of motivating their staff. We asked managers the open-ended question, 'What, in your opinion, is the most effective style of leadership for managers?' Their replies were then coded according to whether

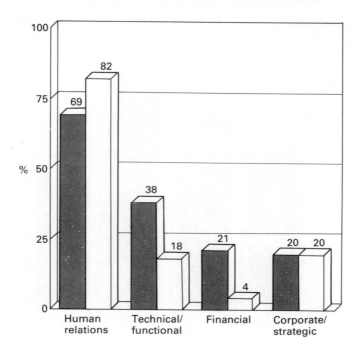

Men

Women

Figure 3.1 Managers' stated training needs.

they were indicative of a preference for 'assertive/directive' or more 'open/consultative' approaches (Tannenbaum and Schmidt, 1958). They were also analysed by reference to the structural characteristics of the managers' work settings; that is, in terms of whether or not they were engaged in more or less bureaucratic structures. Their responses are reported in Figure 3.2.

The following comments, written by managers on the questionnaire schedule, highlight many of the skills which

[69]

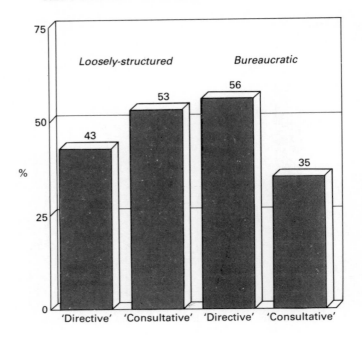

Figure 3.2 Managers' preferences for 'directive' and 'consultative' leadership styles according to organizational setting.

were emphasized by those who favour more directive leadership styles:

> The ability to deal with staff. To be assertive. To emphasize the task oriented factors. To cope with industrial relations problems. (male, early 40s, Finance and Accounting).

> Leadership/motivation. Decision-making and influencing skills. Handling of grievances. Interviewing skills. Self-analysis. Staff reviewing. (male, late 40s, Sales and Marketing).

By contrast, those who profess support for more open and consultative styles describe effective leadership skills in the following terms:

[70]

How to listen; how to counsel; how to motivate; how to support in times of difficulty; how to talk to people; how to share ideas without giving the impression of imposition; how to identify stress in others and help them. (female, late 30s, Finance and Accounting).

Communication skills. How and when to delegate. Using manpower and equipment efficiently. An awareness of subordinates' attitudes; being able to listen to subordinates' inputs. (male, late 20s, Production).

Self-analysis. Communicating skills. Ability to develop motivating skills, to encourage teamwork and to understand people's needs. (male, early 50s, General Management).

What is, perhaps, interesting about these comments is how ideas of managerial effectiveness tend to be loosely associated with the structural characteristics of employing organizations. Those in more highly bureaucratized settings are inclined to stress the advantages of more assertive styles while those in other organizational forms are more likely to emphasize more 'open' and 'consultative' approaches. The tendency for leadership styles and organizational structures to be congruent is possibly derived from features pertaining to the nature of products, technology and skill levels of employees (Bryman, 1986). A reliance on rules and procedures is likely to be evident when work processes can be organized for the purposes of providing relatively standardized goods or services for reasonably stable markets. Those who are performing such tasks rarely need to exercise personal judgement. Hence, patterns of consultation are likely to be restricted to relatively routine matters. This is in sharp contrast to circumstances in those organizations producing complex products and services where highly skilled employees are continually required to exercise responsibility on a day-to-day basis. Under such circumstances, the degree of consultation will be high in conditions where formally prescribed rules and regulations are inappropriate (Mintzberg, 1979). These differences can have important implications for strategies of, and responses to, organizational change. In loosely structured settings, there is likely to be resistance to senior managerial attempts to impose constraints upon flexible and relatively autonomous working practices. Equally, the appeal of bureaucratic models among managers in more highly structured situations is likely to lead them to resist changes in work practices which have, as a consequence, the devolution of responsibilities to junior colleagues (Kanter, 1983). Accordingly, senior managers within these organizations are often only able to innovate within the parameters of prevailing ideals and assumptions. Organizational 'change', then, can often reinforce their bureaucratic attributes which, in turn, may exaggerate the levels of job dissatisfaction experienced by junior colleagues.[9]

Indeed, the mutually reinforcing and interdependent nature of interpersonal skills, leadership styles and organizational structures are reflected in managers' notions of operating effectiveness. In our survey, managers were asked: 'What, in your opinion, is the most appropriate structure for an organization in the 1980s?' Their answers were then coded in terms of their preferences for bureaucratic or more loosely structured organizational forms (Figure 3.3).

Women would seem to be more in favour of clearly defined, rule-bound work settings. In these, there are more visible guidelines and criteria for designating appropriate forms of behaviour whereas in less structured situations, anxieties over their management effectiveness can be reinforced by operating ambiguities.[10] But, in the main, men and women's perceptions of organizational effectiveness do seem to be shaped by their immediate work experiences and, hence, reaffirm the subtle interplay between personal styles and prescribed structures. The following comments reflect the preferences of some of those employed in the more highly bureaucratized organizations:

> It is essential to have set lines of communication and accountability. The immediate manager must be known. A sub-

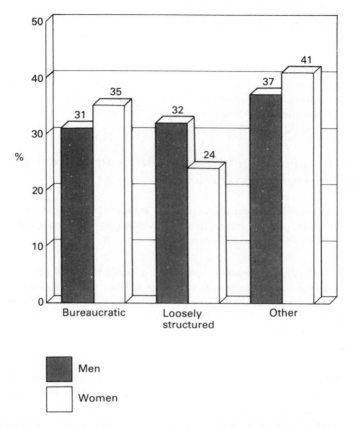

Figure 3.3 Managers' preferences for bureaucratic and loosely structured organizational forms.

ordinate must have one boss. The hierarchy should be pyramid based, with a point at the top. Work must be split between sections . . . without overlap or duplication. (female, early 40s, General Management).

A proper central form of administration without which no organization will function efficiently. Clear lines of communication and responsibility at all levels. Proper and firm direction from senior management. (female, late 40s, Administration).

[73]

Clear accountability with direct lines of communication to line management. (female, late 40s, Administration).

A certain hierarchy of authority is probably inevitable, but this should be as uncomplicated and clear as possible. Lines of communication and areas of responsibility should be clearly defined and there should be sensible but not excessive delegation. (male, early 40s, General Management).

By contrast, those in less formalized settings describe their preferred structures in the following ways:

Decentralized organizations with smaller profit centres to which employees can relate and develop commitment. (male, late 40s, Finance and Accounting).

It is always important . . . to have a dedicated team responsible for such activities as customer relations and communications, with perhaps a matrix structure for areas such as production, quality control and sales. The structure should encourage and allow for personal development . . . through regular discussion. (male, late 30s, Production).

A very low management structure with few steps between the supervisor and the chief executive. The management would be multi-skilled and mobile within the organization . . . no limit on company size in the downward direction but would be in the upward. No central control, with each branch totally accountable for development and profit/loss. (male, early 40s, Engineering and Maintenance).

Decentralized, project based. Despite greater inefficiencies . . . the enhanced teamwork, morale and dedication to specific projects outweighs these. (male, early 30s, General Management).

Small local units of under 100 people each with independent autonomous local management which can react to the needs of customers within an area. All such units to be profit responsible centres. (male, late 30s, General Management).

With large changes in technology and working practices, including automation, it is important that the organization is seen to encourage teamwork and self-motivation whilst allowing the individual access to management. (male, late 30s, Production).

These comments reflect the close interplay that exists between personal preferences and structure and confirm the extent to which organizations, consisting of specific structures, ideals and goals, are capable of shaping the social perspectives of their managers. If, in the past, a major senior managerial strategy for obtaining the compliance of junior colleagues was through structuring organizations according to different bureaucratic models, a growing recognition of the possible dysfunctions of these for motivation and morale has enhanced the potential appeal of alternative organizational forms. However, attempts to achieve greater operational effectiveness through the use of looser structures often leads to resistance among many managers because of their doubts about their ability to manage through face-to-face negotiation and to exercise more *personal* forms of leadership. At the same time they are reluctant to shift from bureaucratic organizational modes of control because the introduction of flexible procedures would require them to be more immersed 'psychologically' in their jobs. Accordingly, it seems unlikely that such structures will be adopted within anything but a limited number of contexts; senior managers in most organizations will continue to adhere to various strategies of bureaucratic control. As such, problems of morale and motivation which they perceive to exist among middle and junior managers are likely to be tackled through limited and piecemeal strategies directed towards the redesign of jobs rather than through more fundamental organizational change. It is in such terms that managerial careers are regarded as important mechanisms of commitment. What, then, is the nature of these within the context of broader organizational settings? We discuss this in the next chapter.

Notes

1   This problem was particularly evident in our own research when it was clear that similar functional specialisms were defined quite differently in terms of their tasks and duties within each of the six organizations.

2   This point is worth emphasizing if only because of the tendency to 'reify' notions of organizational structure such that they are described as possessing properties which are 'beyond' and 'removed' from the influences of participating actors.

3   There has been a 'rediscovery' of organizational cultures in recent years. In most discussions, 'culture' is ambiguously and vaguely defined and, indeed, few social anthropologists would recognize its use in most discussions of organizations as legitimate. For the purposes of the present discussion, we prefer to refer to predominant *values* or *ideals* as these are imposed and sustained by senior managers.

4   Such paradigms are seen to be particularly appropriate for those organizations within which the skill levels of employees are high and the divisions between managerial and non-managerial roles are less pronounced. In traditional manufacturing enterprises where most work tasks are routinized and 'de-skilled', more mechanistic and hierarchical forms of control are likely to prevail.

5   This was evident within the two public sector organizations of our own study. In both, there had been attempts to impose more 'flexible' operating procedures but the subsequent 'confusion' and 'inefficiencies' which these had created were in some cases leading to the reimposition of more formalized methods of control.

6   By this we mean that managers in such organizational settings are able to 'refer to' or 'use' formalized rules and procedures as tools of compliance. In 'looser' structures, they are more compelled to negotiate personally with colleagues in order to get tasks accomplished.

7   'Outsiders' have often been appointed in order to 'turn around' or 'rationalize' public sector industries and organizations and even parts of central and local government.

8   There has been virtually no research on the extent to which gender identities are differently constructed according to various organizational settings.

[76]

9   Hence the need for appointed 'outsiders' for the purposes of implementing more far-reaching structural changes within such organizations.

10 This may partly explain why there are more women managers in public sector organizations where bureaucratic forms of administration are more likely to prevail (Alban-Metcalfe and Nicholson, 1984).

CHAPTER 4

Personal ambitions and careers

The career has been described as the 'supreme social reality' for large sectors of the middle class (Dahrendorf, 1959). In many ways, it constitutes a set of organizing principles around which those in managerial and professional occupations are able to structure both their work and non-work lives. It enables managers, in particular, to make sense of what might otherwise appear as an almost random series of events and activities. Corporate careers, as they have developed during the postwar decades, confer a sense of stability, order and, usually, security (Pahl and Pahl, 1971). Those who have careers typically experience a sense of achievement and advancement largely because their jobs do not simply consist of undertaking tasks on a day-to-day basis, but, instead, are directed to the attainment of longer-term personal goals (Sofer, 1970). Together, the promise of relative job security and the offer of personal advancement within corporate hierarchies represent the major rewards of the twentieth-century middle-class career (Wilensky, 1961). These, as well as financial remuneration, are the key mechanisms whereby large-scale corporations obtain the motivation and commitment of their managerial employees. By contrast, other categories of employees are noticeably less well paid and secure in their jobs, and their commitment to organizational goals is often relatively limited.

However, as we have suggested, a number of organizational, technological and social changes during the closing decades of the century are combining to undermine career rewards and to create circumstances in which many managers, particularly at middle and junior levels, are being forced to reconsider their traditional assumptions about, and attitudes towards, work. In this chapter we explore the new ways in which they regard their careers in the light of changing corporate structures which may be offering them fewer opportunities for personal advancement and less job security. In particular, we discuss how the meaning of career success is changing and how those whose expectations may be frustrated are able to cope with their feelings of personal failure. But before considering these processes, it is worth restating the basic characteristics of the typical organizational career of the 1950s and 1960s.[1]

Traditionally, the managerial career is alleged to consist of a 'meaningful' progression through a series of related jobs. This is expected to occur in a relatively routine manner, if only because of the essentially hierarchical nature of large-scale bureaucratic organizations. The criteria for advancement are often varied but normally incorporate considerations to do with length of service, ability and performance. As managers are mobile within such hierarchies, they are rewarded with enhanced income, status and security. Many of the studies conducted in the 1950s and 1960s stress the fundamental significance of this promotion process in the work and non-work experiences of corporate managers. In his study of middle-level executives in the oil, motor manufacturing and chemical industries, for example, Sofer (1970) found that 'the men were preoccupied with promotion . . . Nine out of every ten men we interviewed took up the question of their promotion chances at some point . . . Past moves and decisions were discussed largely in terms of their implications for promotion. When asked directly about their wishes for the future, at least three quarters of the men made it clear that they wanted to "move up"!' (p.309). Similarly, the Pahls (1971) noted that 'Middle managers in British industry appear to be willing slaves to the system . . . For them, life is a hierarchy and success means moving up in it.

[79]

Marking time and staying in the same position is interpreted as dropping out' (p.259).

Why have managers traditionally attached such importance to promotion? For some, particularly those in lower-level positions, the expected rewards of the 'next job' have been a major justification for accepting the dissatisfactions of their present duties. For others, promotion has been the only route whereby they can increase their earnings and maximize their material returns from work. This is in sharp contrast to some other occupational groups who, without promotion, are able to obtain bonuses, commissions and various productivity-related payments. But, for managers, there are also less tangible but psychologically important benefits derived from the identity conferring properties of career progression.[2] Managers, like many others, tend to describe *who* they are in terms of *what* they do; in other words, their self-images are traditionally derived from their jobs. But their sense of progression between jobs has further consequences for the shaping of their personal identities because it gives meaning to both their past and potential future working experiences. Again, to quote Sofer (1970) writing in the 1960s, managers within large-scale corporations come to 'base their self-conceptions on the assumption that, in due course, they will be what the institution allows persons to be' (p.36). Thus, career success, measured through promotion, reaffirms the value of past endeavours and sustains the prospects of future progression. It therefore encourages individuals to view their working experiences as part of a meaningful process of personality development. As a result, personal 'success' or 'failure' becomes measured according to occupational accomplishments rather than in terms of criteria associated with various non-work achievements.

It is, then, not surprising that notions of personal success tend to be closely linked with various age-related 'stages'. If individuals have achieved particular positions within organizational hierarchies by a particular age, then they should feel satisfied. If they 'arrive' early there is additional psychological

[80]

reward, while if they 'arrive' late or became 'stuck', there can be personal anxiety and frustration. Thus, various models (Hall, 1976; Hunt and Collins, 1983; Schein, 1978) of careers within organizations refer to an 'exploratory' stage until the mid-20s when individuals experiment with a variety of occupations and test different career options. This is followed by a 'building' phase which lasts until the mid-30s when career routes became more firmly established. From then until the mid-40s there follows a period of 'evaluation' when past achievements are reviewed and, in the light of this, future possibilities are assessed. Finally, there is a stage of 'consolidation' when individuals come to terms with their achieved occupational positions and are primarily concerned to optimize their experiences of job satisfaction. Of course, the timing of such stages can vary according to a range of personal, occupational, organizational and industrial factors, all of which shape the precise trajectory and speed of particular personal careers (Hunt, 1986). None the less, in broad terms, those in careers tend to pass through these phases and, psychologically, to structure their personal biographies accordingly.

In view of the changing nature of work organizations, however, it may seem necessary to query many of the assumptions underlying this model. Fewer managers are now likely to enjoy 'orderly', predictable career paths within bureaucratically structured organizations. Shifts within some organizations towards decentralization and attempts to develop 'task-oriented ideals' mean that managers are increasingly required to work within smaller, self-contained, semi-autonomous units which, in order to be 'flexible' and 'responsive', are designed to avoid rigid, bureaucratic hierarchies (Kanter, 1983). Further, the increased risks of redundancy force managers to reappraise their traditional assumptions of uninterrupted, lifelong career paths (Berthoud, 1979). Some are compelled, in mid-life, to retrain and embark upon entirely new careers while others have to be content with early retirement (Handy, 1984; Wood, 1980).

[81]

After pursuing careers within large corporations an increasing number may become self-employed, start their own small businesses or become involved with management buy-outs (Scase and Goffee, 1987). Hence, the new-found appeal of proprietorship and the spread of more flexible, contractual and consultancy-based work relationships.[3] Taken together, such developments query many of the postwar assumptions about orderly managerial careers within large-scale, hierarchical organizations. For many managers, these may now represent but one of a variety of work experiences (Hearn, 1977). Increasingly, they are encouraged to 'manage their own careers' and, as a result, to contemplate more frequent moves between organizations as well as between employment and self-employment, instead of enjoying lifelong careers within a single corporation (Nicholson and Alban-Metcalfe, 1988). Under such circumstances, it becomes more difficult for managers to plan their own career routes and, indeed, to compare their 'actual' with 'expected' progress. Thus, as career paths become less certain, attempts to categorize personal progress neatly into a series of age-related stages becomes more problematic. In effect, the early 'exploratory' phase becomes drastically extended as managers experiment with different work options in less predictable organizational settings. But if this marks a significant change for men, the careers of women have traditionally been less orderly and routine because of their husbands' own career paths, their family and domestic obligations and the associated tendency for many employers to assume they have only limited ambitions (Marshall, 1984).

Linked with these developments we would suggest that there have been related changes in the attitudes of many managers. Fewer would now seem to be committed to career success, at least in the ways in which it has been conventionally understood. Personal achievement and life satisfaction are probably less likely to be solely equated with promotion within organizational structures; instead, career advancement is seen as a means of enhancing personal lifestyles which are separated from, rather than subordinated to, work roles (Evans and Bartholomé, 1980). This is not to suggest that managers no longer view their careers as important or continue to aspire to higher positions; plainly, many of them do. However, in the context of increased competition for a diminishing number of opportunities at senior managerial levels, they are less prepared to sacrifice their 'selves' or make the kind of open-ended commitments which might harm their domestic lifestyles. Conceptions of *personal* success have become more broadly defined in that they incorporate non-work criteria according to which the costs and benefits of career success are measured. In short, fewer managers may now be reliably regarded as 'organization men', fully prepared to act as 'willing slaves to the system' in ways depicted by observers in the 1960s (Pahl and Pahl, 1971; Whyte, 1965).

As we have already pointed out in Chapter 2, managers are well aware of their reduced promotion prospects, and for many this represents an important reason for their declining job satisfaction. Indeed, only four in ten of both men and women in our survey express any optimism about their future career prospects. In the face of these diminished promotion opportunities, the frustration of younger, junior managers is often particularly acute:

> I think that I, in my career, and other people at my level, face a period of great stagnation. Promotion opportunities will be limited for the foreseeable future . . . That's really because of the organizational changes . . . I am very concerned about my future promotion opportunities – particularly in the next five years. I'm not the most patient of men and, like most people, I think I should be further advanced in my career than I actually am . . . The latest corporate cock-up is a further block to promotion . . . In the end, you get frustrated. Not only would I benefit financially from promotion but the bank would benefit by stretching me a little more. I feel I'm underutilized in my present job. (male, late 20s, Finance and Accounting).

I am beginning to feel that I could do with a move, a change. Before I did this job, which I've been in for four years, I'd not have a job much longer than nine months. I've always moved from one job to another in a fast moving environment . . . if I don't move in the next two or three years, I shall feel severely constrained . . . But it's a matter of availability . . . There are a lot of young people like me who enjoy their jobs and want to get the next job up the ladder. But the growth of the early 1970s has slowed down . . . There aren't the jobs, there aren't the opportunities. It's a big problem. (male, late 20s, General Management).

These views are typical of younger managers who wish to advance their careers but who work within organizations where employment and promotion opportunities are static, if not contracting. Middle-aged and older managers in similar circumstances are more likely to accept that they have reached a plateau and to search for alternative sources of self-fulfilment outside employment. In our survey, for example, about half of all those aged between 46 and 55 had not been promoted in the previous five years. Fully 30 per cent of the men and 50 per cent of the women in this age group say they have reached the height of their career aspirations. Amongst men *over* 55, the equivalent figure is 57 per cent. By contrast, only 1 per cent of men and 4 per cent of women in the 26–35 age group say that their present position is the highest to which they aspire. But those younger managers who have invested heavily – often through education – in preparation for their careers are now forced to compete for positions which, in the past, they could have assumed they would achieve almost 'automatically'.[4] Yet, even here, there may be a careful evaluation of the costs involved in career pursuit and, in particular, the possible adverse effects which these can have on personal and family lives. As one of them explains:

I've gone past the point of no return now. I'm very nearly 30 years of age and I've been in the bank eleven years. I'm happy with the way I've progressed to date and I think there's a long-term career . . . But there are fewer opportunities now and it will probably get worse in years to come. Now if there's a post available and there are two people going for it, you've got to make sure you're better. So, in some ways, for those who are keen and ambitious, this new situation will drive people a bit harder. It will make them improve their performance and their standards . . . I'm just going to have to prove that I'm better than the rest to make sure I reach senior positions . . . I'll try to push myself as far as I can go so long as I can cope . . . With a job that's too much for me or where my family life would suffer, well, there's no point, is there? You might have the salary and the perks that go with the job, but if there's a lot of pressure, there's no point. It's better to be on one plane lower and enjoy life and be happy in your job. (male, late 20s, Finance and Accounting).

Women managers also perceive growing discrepancies between their career aspirations and the available opportunities. This, in many ways, has always been a feature of their labour market experiences, if only because career paths have been structured according to the expectations of men rather than women. As a consequence, women have been forced to adapt to restricted opportunities by becoming *job* rather than *career* oriented: concerned with the immediate, intrinsic rewards of their tasks at hand rather than with future, long-term career benefits (Marshall, 1984). It is almost as if any promotion which they do obtain is regarded as an unanticipated additional bonus. Women managers, then, may be less inclined to construct career plans consciously because they are more accustomed to unpredictable work experiences. If, for example, careers are blocked by the prejudices of male colleagues, interrupted by pregnancy and child rearing or by their partners' own career moves then it is hardly surprising that they do not set 'unrealistic' expectations for themselves. Indeed, their attitudes may be more compatible with present-day organizational conditions than those of some men who remain committed to long-term 'orderly' careers. The less explicitly planned and discontinuous nature of women's

[85]

career experiences is illustrated by the following reflections:

I've never actually thought of myself as a career woman. It's only in the last couple of years because other people have said, 'She's a career woman', that I've actually thought in those terms. I certainly never intended to be one . . . I mean, I don't have a burning ambition for a long-term future. I don't have some long-term goal. I have short-term things that I want to do . . . if something suddenly altered my life dramatically, it wouldn't bother me. (female, late 20s, General Management).

When I joined the organization, I saw it as a job. I didn't think of the possibility of a career . . . I didn't see myself as a 'computer person' or a 'corporate person' or whatever . . . I always wanted to be independent and to support myself . . . but I didn't have the goal of 'management' in my mind as a career, although I suppose, indirectly, that's what I was aiming for . . . I'm not career orientated, I'm more orientated to some sort of challenge – something new and interesting. That's what motivates me. (female, late 30s, General Management).

There does come a point when you begin to see people younger than you coming up and overtaking. At that point, you've got to decide if you want to go flat out and keep pace with them or call a halt. I want to do something I enjoy doing. I want to do something I do well . . . I like to actually get on and do things. I like to feel I'm having an impact. Not just setting down what's going to happen and leaving it for someone else to do . . . a lot of people who have rapid promotions eventually get stuck in a job where, nine times out of ten, they're less happy than with the one they've already got. I'm not into that. I enjoy what I'm doing now. There's still some ambition there. I would still like to get further. But I'm not sure whether it's going to be a straight line upwards or a sideways stagger! (female, late 30s, Finance and Accounting).

When you talk to men and in the literature you read – they seem to say, 'My career involves doing this and doing that and then doing the other.' But I'd rather just take things as they come, I'm afraid. I don't have a sort of 'big plan'. I've never

[86]

really envisaged where my life would end up. I'm quite happy to turn round and go wherever an interesting avenue opens . . . I'm only as successful as I've been because of the effort I've felt prepared to make. But a career is not the be-all and end-all of my life in any way. (female, early 30s, Engineering and Development).

Despite the uncertainty surrounding career opportunities for both men and women, some managers, of course, are still being promoted. But what are the individual qualities and skills which they need in order to be successful in their careers? How are these seen to have altered as a result of organizational restructuring over recent years? A variety of attributes, abilities and behaviours are often used to explain differences in individual career achievement. Indeed, in Chapter 3 we discussed some of these by reference to managers' preferred personality characteristics and leadership styles. But these, alone, are insufficient explanation of why, in career terms, some are relatively more successful than others. Clearly, there are many factors involved. For those pursuing *occupational* careers, for example, professional qual-ifications and other kinds of performance-related achieve-ments are likely to be particularly important. In effect, they serve as 'proof' of individual abilities and expertise which can be applied in a variety of organizational contexts. Those in *organizational* careers, on the other hand, may place consider-able emphasis upon 'loyalty', 'reliability' and 'commitment'; qualities which, almost by definition, evolve gradually through lengthy service for a single employer (Brown, 1982; Crompton and Sanderson, 1986). In addition to these factors, there are a variety of social and political skills which are often seen as important. These help individuals, so it is claimed, to ensure contacts and, through careful positioning, seize what might appear as 'chance' opportunities (Jay, 1967; Mangham, 1986). In our survey we asked managers to indicate the extent to which they regarded these kinds of factors as important determinants of career success; their responses are summar-ized in Figure 4.1.

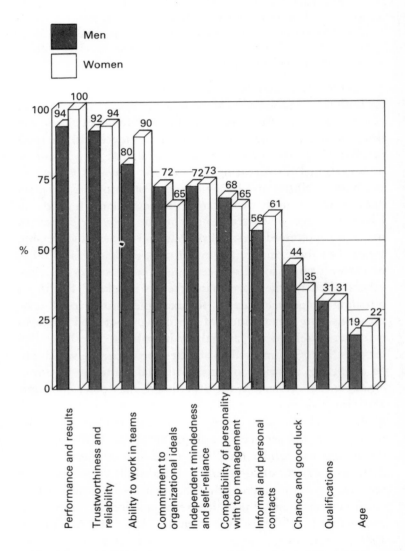

Figure 4.1 Managers' perceptions of the importance of various factors shaping career success (percentage assessing factors as 'important' or 'very important').

Clearly there is substantial agreement amongst managers about which are the key factors. Perhaps not surprisingly, the great majority perceive 'performance and results' to be the major determinants of career success. There is, however, recognition of the importance of various non-meritocratic criteria and what might broadly be described as organizational 'acceptability'. A clear majority claim that the display of 'trustworthiness', 'reliability', 'commitment' and 'compatibility with senior management' are important for pursuing their careers (Kanter, 1977). Although many middle and junior managers are subject to tight control and accountability they are expected to subscribe formally to certain corporate ideals.[5] Consequently, those who are ambitious may only be promoted if they can demonstrate to those in senior positions that they are 'committed' and 'trustworthy'. This can be particularly important in more loosely structured organizations because of the relative absence of rules and clearly prescribed procedures (Mintzberg, 1979). In these circumstances, managers are especially subject to pressures to uphold the ideals of their employing organizations. This can involve explicitly subscribing to the attitudes, opinions, beliefs and even the personal interests of senior managers. Although, to some extent, such attitudes can be acquired through a process of organizational socialization, the criteria for personal 'acceptability' and 'compatibility' can often only be obtained through having encountered particular educational and childhood experiences. Accordingly, we would argue that social-class background may be considered an implicit but nevertheless more relevant factor shaping 'acceptability' than solely the possession of specific educational and technical qualifications (Whitley and Marceau, 1981). The latter, alone, do not guarantee the trustworthiness and reliability which senior managers often consider as especially important when promoting their junior colleagues.

It is for these reasons that many women feel disadvantaged in their careers. So few have reached positions of seniority that the criteria for determining their commitment and trustworthiness are ill-defined (Kanter, 1977). Women tend not to have progressed through educational and career experiences of the sort familiar to those of most male senior managers. At the same time, they are often excluded from 'informal' networks of communication which can be vital for the purposes of managerial decision-making. Since these are generally male-controlled they often lack access to important information and, as such, are disadvantaged in their attempts to perform as competently as their male colleagues (Rothwell, 1985). Accordingly, they can become relatively isolated within many organizations with their credibility subject to scrutiny and their trustworthiness and commitment regarded as doubtful. As one of them told us:

> When I went to the first area meeting to meet senior colleagues, I couldn't help noticing . . . that they would look at me with hostility. The first time I went there, my presence was virtually ignored . . . I could never quite come to terms with that. Initially, I thought they were making fun of me . . . They made remarks like, 'We won't be able to tell any dirty jokes now we've got a woman in our midst.' I may as well have been a spaceman! And they were reluctant to discuss matters of importance with me . . . They would sneer and snigger and whisper behind your back . . . I may just as well have been a cardboard cut-out, initially . . . I feel isolated. I don't feel I can telephone my counterparts for assistance. Whereas I know there's an old boy network amongst the men and that they do telephone around and get to know inside information . . . I don't think I'll ever be able to break into it . . . I ignore it most of the time because it's not important to me . . . I detach myself a bit, I suppose, by the fact that I am excluded. (female, late 30s, Accounting and Finance).

In this context, it is perhaps not surprising that women managers often place particular emphasis upon the need to 'over-achieve'. As such, they feel the need to demonstrate their competence according to various explicit measures of performance. But this, in turn, leads many to feel that

[90]

they are subject to especially close scrutiny (Davidson and Cooper, 1983). The following comment is typical:

> People seem to watch female managers very closely. There is less opportunity to perform at will. It's almost a situation where people expect you to prove over and over again that you are able to do the job rather than being left to get on with it. (female, early 30s, Sales and Marketing).

Men and women managers feel, then, that to be successful in their careers, they must appear reliable, trustworthy, committed *and* capable of achieving consistently high levels of work performance. Those who can 'deliver' may be duly rewarded but those who cannot are no longer guaranteed comfortable security until retirement. Of course, career structures within formal hierarchies have always ensured that progression to the top is strictly limited to a small minority. But during the growth and prosperity of the 1950s and 1960s there were more opportunities and, indeed, greater scope to 'disguise' lack of achievement (Pahl and Pahl, 1971). In the 1980s, 'winners' and 'losers' tend to be more clearly differentiated and, while the former are offered special 'fast track' personal development programmes and carefully planned job moves, the latter are increasingly left, implicitly and explicitly, to 'manage their own careers'.[6] This may be difficult in the context of reduced promotion prospects and increased risks of redundancy.

How, then, do those managers cope who feel they have limited prospects? Much, of course, will depend upon their personal circumstances as shaped by age, marketable skills, family commitments and so on. Their responses will also be influenced by the various corporate career paths within which they are located. Those in 'low ceiling' jobs, for example, are unlikely to anticipate much upward movement within corporate hierarchies (Kanter, 1977). 'Getting stuck' on these short ladders is normally less psychologically painful than it is for those who, having expected substantial mobility, have simply 'lost out' as opportunities have become more uncertain. Among the latter, many will begin to question the calibre of their particular talents and skills. Some may become embittered because they feel their efforts and achievements have been inadequately recognized (Hunt and Collins, 1983). This may be particularly the case for those who have been previously sponsored and trained for senior corporate positions. The psychological adjustments involved may be painful and can lead to individuals changing companies, shifting jobs, embarking upon quite different careers and, even, experimenting with business start-ups (Scase and Goffee, 1987). Most, however, are forced to redefine their work expectations. If, at an earlier age, they perceived their jobs as integral components of longer term career paths, this ceases to be the case. Some begin to see their jobs less as a means for promotion and personal development and more as a source of financial security. Yet even this can no longer be guaranteed, as the following comments from men in mid-career vividly illustrate:

> At middle management level, there just isn't a lot of movement – it's pretty static . . . to be honest with you, in the back of my mind is the fact that the world is changing fast and although I've been lucky to be with a reasonably secure organisation, I certainly wouldn't want to put money on the fact that I'm going to enjoy the same situation in five years' time. An awful lot can happen in five years . . . Everything shrieks to me that if I'm going to make a change in my life, now is the time to do it because I'm young enough to take it on. But, in the back of my mind is always the longing for total security . . . Nothing is for ever, nothing is for sure and, yes, I've had it pretty good. I can't really complain. But I would like to feel I was totally secure. (male, late 30s, Production).

> I honestly don't know what's going to happen. I could ask my regional personnel manager tomorrow, 'Where am I going next?' and he wouldn't know either. He wouldn't be able to tell me honestly that in another year or two I should move up the ladder again . . . Five years ago, I was moving every couple of years . . . But now, I don't know where it's

going . . . It's all uncertain . . . I've got two boys doing exams at school, so I'm in for a period of immobility. I can't move to another area, but I don't think there are the opportunities anyway . . . It's being rationalized all over . . . there are a number of people surplus to requirements now . . . I've got a job at the moment, but I can see the time coming when people will say, 'Well, he's been there a number of years, perhaps we should swop him for somebody else'. . . I take stock of things every so often . . . and what it does to me is emphasize again and again that I'm not in control of where I'm going or what I'm doing next. It's really unsatisfactory. (male, early 40s, Administration).

I'm disappointed with myself for not pushing myself further to move on. I shouldn't still be in this job. I should have moved. Sideways or diagonally or something! But it's very easy to get into a rut . . . I'm not optimistic about my future. I'm still confused as to where to go . . . I don't know what position would suit me within the company – maybe I'll just have to live with that . . . I'm comfortable for the time being but it may be that, eventually, I'll have to leave the company and do something totally different. (male, early 40s, General Management).

With promotion opportunities less well defined and prospects uncertain, individuals may be forced to review their careers seriously. Amongst a minority, resentment and depression can lead to 'mid-career crisis' characterized by sub-clinical stress symptoms including insomnia, headaches and an increase in drug dependency and alcohol consumption (Cooper, 1980). Some experience domestic crises which result in marital break-up and divorce (Evans and Bartholomé, 1980). The psychological outcomes of failure, then, can be severe for partners; the wives of male managers may also feel they have 'failed' because the expectations which they had of their husbands' careers have been unfulfilled (Finch, 1983). Managers' anxieties may be reinforced by various organizational pressures which compel them to hide their psychological injuries and continue to perform their jobs in an apparently confident and assertive manner. Consequently, certain kinds of career-related stress among them may be concealed. As one personnel manager observes:

> The tendency is that most people won't admit it. They won't admit defeat. It's very difficult to get people to be open about their personal thoughts . . . then someone who has been a model employee – all of a sudden, something happens . . . when people are under pressure, they tend not to take notice of their colleagues. So things like alcohol and stress are not picked up until something quite significant happens. People keep their heads down and try and get on with the job. They want to see it to the bitter end – they won't get up and move when they see the whole thing crashing down on top of them. It causes a lot of worry but they tend not to express that worry . . . It gets worse as you cut back on people. Those that aren't pulling their weight get shown up more and more . . . I kept getting pestered to do something about one guy. He eventually went off sick and I did some informal digging. I found out that two weeks before he went off sick, he was sitting on his seat in a pool of vomit. But people just kept their heads down – they didn't want to know . . . If you talk to people in my kind of job in other industries, they'd tell you the same thing . . . There's a lot of cases bordering on schizophrenia but we don't pay enough attention to them. (male, late 20s, Personnel).

Managers, then, may go to great lengths to hide their disappointments. Sometimes they, and colleagues who are confronted with similar problems, nurture informal drinking groups which, at lunchtimes and after work, help them to compensate for self-perceived failure. Others seek refuge in workplace sub-cultures that value humour, colleague friendship and 'non-work' interests above promotion and personal career success. In this way they can create more meaningful social worlds. Feeling that they are locked into organizations with few or no promotion prospects, they cope by developing survival strategies which allow them to come to terms with the reality of failure in their careers. But doubts and frustration often remain, as the following account illustrates:

> Looking back on my past, I'm satisfied with the way that things have progressed . . . but I've reached a sort of crossroads in my career. I'm half way through my working life. I've done twenty odd years and I've another twenty to go and it's this which concerns me. Where do I go from here? I don't feel as though I've got too great a future . . . I don't want to be in this job for another twenty years. I would feel as though I was getting into a rut. I am in a rut, quite honestly . . . and the thought of facing another twenty years in this job appals me . . . It's been an interesting career but it's come to an end now. That's basically it . . . I'm in that middle age bracket, 40 to 45 . . . I've still got a fresh mind, an enquiring mind. I would like to take off. But the financial dependence stops me really. You have a mortgage and you have family responsibilities . . . Quite a few people in the office are disgruntled. Like myself, they feel as though their time has come . . . It's run out for them. But they've got to stick with it. There's no alternative. They're resigned to it . . . With these consultants in, I may be one of the chosen few to go – who knows. I don't know how I would cope, quite honestly. I could probably make a go of something else, but, in your early 40s, it isn't easy. Your ideas have run out, your opportunities have run out, and I've talked too much! (male, early 40s, Finance and Accounting).

As we discussed in Chapter 2 some are able to adapt by investing very little of themselves in their work and merely performing their jobs to an acceptable minimum standard. As we have said, this kind of role-playing is often more feasible in bureaucratic rather than in less formalized structures. In the latter, there are fewer rules and regulations and, as a result, 'acceptable' standards of conduct are less easily established. It is, then, more difficult to minimize efforts and those who attempt to disengage themselves psychologically are more likely to be seen as 'unco-operative' and 'uncommitted'. However, such work settings may offer more opportunities for self-development *within* jobs so that managers are less

[95]

likely to feel that they are locked into rigidly defined roles since there remain greater opportunities, even for those with limited career prospects, to develop new initiatives and ventures (Morgan, 1986). It is possible, then, for individuals to experience a renewed sense of achievement and personal worth through internal job development; they are less likely to feel that their talents are underutilized as they seek ways for enlarging their own work experiences. One manager gives an indication of this flexibility as follows:

> Although there may not be opportunities . . . I think it's a state of mind . . . In this company, it's continual change and continual challenge . . . There's little chance of becoming bored or stagnating. There's so much to do. Looking ahead, I can see all these challenges . . . Some people regard change as a problem they can't come to grips with. For me, it's not an enormous mountain. It's an opportunity to do other things. (male, early 30s, Sales and Marketing).

This kind of attitude occurs less frequently among managers whose promotion opportunities are blocked within more tightly structured, bureaucratic organizations. For them, personal development and career success are more directly equated with promotion. This often leads to feelings that they have been cheated; organizations which once promised them futures are now seen to have reneged on their responsibilities. Having invested perhaps ten or twenty years of their working lives for their companies and having established identities centred on their careers, they feel unable or unwilling to search for alternatives. Although a small number may change jobs or leave, many resolve to extract what they are 'owed' by instrumentally taking as much as they can, in terms of salaries and fringe benefits, and giving, in return, as little effort as possible. One manager describes the change in his colleagues' attitudes in this way:

> All banks have traditionally thrived on the loyalty of their staff . . . but as the bank becomes more commercial in its dealing with staff, they become more commercial in their

attitude towards the employer. They take the view, for example, of 'Well, if I'm not feeling 100 per cent today, why should I go in?' So, I can see the loyalty disappearing eventually. The average member of staff, they'll do their jobs, get their salary and that's it. There's no career attached to it. As long as they get their salary and their holidays, they're not going to worry much, you see . . . the terms of employment have changed because circumstances have changed. (male, early 40s, Administration).

In extreme cases, managers are not content simply to do this. Instead, they develop various 'anti-organizational' attitudes which can seriously undermine the morale and efforts of their colleagues. Thus, new initiatives are greeted with cynicism and proposals for changes in working practices resisted. In these contexts attempts by senior managers to emphasize the importance of corporate ideals may be viewed as a strategy intended, at least in part, to counter the low level of motivation derived from unfulfilled career expectations. However, the success of such strategies is likely to be limited, if only because, increasingly, these managers are inclined to divert their energies into interests and relationships *outside* work (Pym, 1986). An indication of this is given in their evaluation of the significance of various aspects of their lives in terms of personal satisfaction. In order to assess the relative importance which they attach to various work and non-work activities the managers in our study were asked to rank the relative priorities of their jobs, career achievements, family and personal relationships, leisure pursuits and home-based activities. Their responses are summarized in Figure 4.2.

From Figure 4.2 it is clear that most male managers rank 'family and personal relationships' above 'career achievements' as the most important source of life satisfaction. The declining significance of career achievements is further reflected in the fact that no more than 20 per cent even rank these as second in their scale of priorities. Among women managers, on the other hand, fewer are likely to give priority to family and personal relationships and more are inclined to

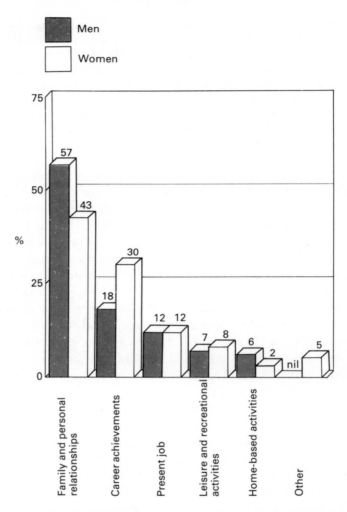

Figure 4.2 Major sources of satisfaction in life (percentage of men and women managers ranking each factor as 'most satisfying').

regard their career achievements as the major source of personal satisfaction. Although such gender differences can be linked to the lower proportion of women managers who are married, it must be recognized that they are usually confronted with greater obstacles in their working careers. If, then, they are successful in achieving their personal work-related goals, this is likely to be a more psychologically rewarding experience.

As far as men are concerned, there appears to have been a shift in their personal priorities over recent decades. Our data would seem to confirm that men's unfulfilled career expectations, their increasing frustrations associated with programmes of organizational restructuring and the continuous redesign of their jobs are leading them to withdraw psychologically from work and to seek greater personal rewards in their private lives. Indeed, their changing attitudes are, perhaps, best summed up by their responses to one question in our survey which assessed whether they agree that 'the personal costs of career pursuit outweigh the benefits'. Only 35 per cent of the men positively disagree with this statement by comparison with 61 per cent of the women. These attitudes contrast strongly with those of the 1960s when, for example, Sofer (1970) in his study of (male) managers was able to conclude that they

> see their jobs as playing a large part in their lives . . .[on] a scale ranging at the one end from experiencing the job as a dominant feature of one's life and a primary source of satisfaction to perception of the job as a source of demand that threatens other activities . . . The majority . . . are towards the dominance–primary source of satisfaction end of the scale. (p.213).

Similarly, despite some reservations, the Pahls (1971) concluded that the (male) managers in their 1960s study 'see work as a central life-interest' (p.259). Our survey, conducted in the mid-1980s, paints a rather different picture. Confronted with diminishing career prospects, managers are no longer prepared to 'sell themselves' to their employing corporations at the expense of their families and their personal leisure interests. Although this might be expected with older managers, it is, perhaps, surprising that a similar pattern is found among their younger colleagues. As Figure 4.3 indicates, they, too, would seem to be restructuring their life interests and, in doing so, confirming our view that work and career are of declining personal importance. Alternatively, they could be embarking upon careers with little or no conception that their employment will offer them psychologically rewarding experiences. If so, such a pattern would be distinctly different from that expected in studies conducted in earlier postwar decades.

Managers of all ages, then, seem concerned to improve the quality of their personal lifestyles outside rather than within work (Robertson, 1985). While some may become involved in different forms of community activity, others pursue a variety of more home-based hobbies and leisure interests. In these ways, they reduce their psychological dependency upon their work roles and consciously cultivate non-work identities. As a result, even those in their late 40s or early 50s may already be attracted to taking early retirement and may be planning, accordingly, the appropriate strategies. By comparison, in the past, managers were more emotionally committed to their jobs and, as such, retirement was often seen as a form of 'premature death' with many experiencing difficulties in adjusting to non-work lifestyles (Hunt and Collins, 1983). In the 1980s, however, more seemed prepared for such lifestyles because they have consciously reduced their psychological dependence upon employment. As one manager admits:

> The emphasis I place on work is changing for a number of reasons. It's to do with the perception of a career, how much commitment there is, the state of the psychological contract, all that sort of thing. I've been at work now for 31 years and that's one hell of a long sentence. I'm beginning to look at ways of putting it to my advantage because once you realize you are never going to be Prime Minister, you really are looking for how you can get the best experience and balance in your life. And the quality of life is becoming increasingly important . . . We live this fairly simple life, fairly unsophisti-

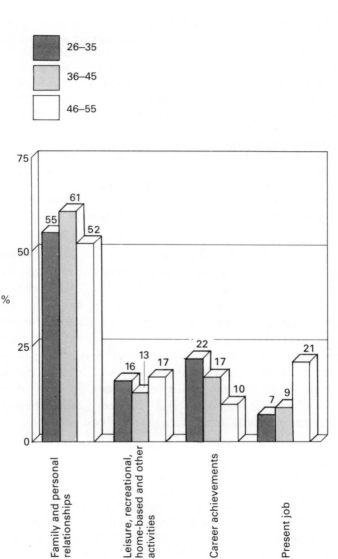

Figure 4.3 Major sources of satisfaction in life according to age group (percentage of men managers rating each factor as 'most satisfying').

cated. We don't need or have many aspirations for gran-
deur . . . Not living in a town, you're basically aware of the
seasons and it gives you a tremendous amount of pleasure . . .
On super days, one's really saying, 'What's the point in
cutting yourself off from all this?' You know, if you're going
to go on and take a more complicated job that means more
hours, more fatigue, less enjoyment. It's getting out of
balance . . . After two or three years, the point will come
where I'll say to them, 'Look, enough's enough. I can survive
without your salary – give me the pension and off I'll go . . .'
The situation's changed. The Protestant ethic is really wearing
a bit thin. To me and my contemporaries, it seems a bit of a
joke . . . We realize it simply isn't necessary to work on until
you're 60 or 65. (male, late 40s, General Management).

In fact, very few of the managers in our survey want to
work until the formally prescribed retirement age; two-thirds
express a firm desire to retire in their 50s.[7] All of them are
employed by organizations which offer relatively generous
early retirement schemes and many admit that their primary
reason for continuing to stay in their jobs is in order to retire
early with maximum benefits. Undoubtedly, the popularity
of such schemes among older managers is directly related to
their growing preferences for 'opting out' in view of their
work-related frustrations and limited career prospects
(McGoldrick, 1983). One of them sums it up as follows:

When they introduced the retirement scheme, they were
absolutely staggered by the number of managers who applied.
It just got out of control. So they had to say, 'Right, we'll
only take the ones we fancy'. . . I think it's a good thing . . .
after 55, people get tired and I don't think they can cope with
the type of pressure they're under, what's demanded of them
today . . . Towards the end of your span, you should be able
to have the time and energy to do something you enjoy. So
many people are just worked out physically . . . people in
their late 50s and 60s shouldn't have to cope with what they
have, they shouldn't have to cope with this sort of business.
(male, late 40s, Finance and Accounting).

[102]

But what of those managers who feel they are locked into their jobs and are too young to take early retirement? A small number may choose to retrain in order to pursue quite contrasting employment opportunities. They may, for example, take up teaching or social work or opt simply for employment which minimizes their need, for example, to commute to, or work in, large impersonal organizations. Those in mid-life may reassess their careers at this stage, when children may have left home, mortgage repayments are concluding and wives may be returning to work. As their financial commitments diminish they are able to review the costs and benefits of their jobs and to take decisions accordingly.

But for their younger colleagues, business start-up has become increasingly popular (Goffee and Scase, 1985, Scase and Goffee, 1987). Whereas amongst managers in the 1960s, according to the Pahls (1971), 'It was rare for anyone [managers] to have ambitions for themselves to have, or for their children to have, their own business or organization' (p.261), the appeal of entrepreneurship has grown dramatically in the 1980s. Of those in our survey, for example, no fewer than 59 per cent of the men and 55 per cent of the women have contemplated starting their own businesses. Among those men under 35 as many as 70 per cent have considered business start-up compared with just under half of those aged over 45. Typically, it is those who remain career-oriented, who are frustrated by their lack of promotion opportunities and who feel their talents and abilities are underutilized in their jobs, who are most likely to consider self-employment as an alternative work strategy (Scase and Goffee, 1986). The following comments are typical of many younger men and women managers:

> If, by my late 30s, I haven't reached the higher echelons, I will be looking for a business opportunity for me personally, as opposed to working for somebody else . . . I'm attracted by the independence . . . most of us in this industry are entre-preneurial businessmen trying to get out. But we tend

sometimes to be constrained by the company we work for. We find we have to work within certain guidelines . . . I've got to the sort of age where, given the opportunity, it would be worth a gamble. (male, early 30s, Sales and Marketing).

My next move is being blocked, so I don't know what happens next. I've had, for a little while, a hankering that if I don't do my own thing by 40, I'm going to lose out. I've had an idea sort of bubbling in my mind for a little while, to do something on my own . . . This block has rekindled the idea to do a little test marketing and go it alone . . . It could be the shove I need. (female, late 30s, Research and Development).

Of course, those who translate these aspirations into reality remain, at present, a very small minority. Even so, the evidence suggests that, overall, their numbers are growing. Between the mid-1960s and the mid-1980s, for example, the numbers of self-employed in Britain increased by almost 60 per cent (Bannock, 1987). As we discussed in Chapter 3, some large corporations are attempting to retain the talents and energies of their managers by decentralizing their structures and encouraging the development of more autonomous management teams which are encouraged to be entrepreneurial. Other senior managers have offered their staff opportunities to 'buy out' parts of their operations; indeed, these have increased fivefold during the past decade (Bannock, 1987). But while these represent, in many ways, relatively radical attempts to alleviate the problems faced by those locked within conventional career structures, it is difficult to envisage such changes having a substantial impact on the circumstances of most middle managers. As such, there will continue to be a stratum of managers, like those quoted above, who although attracted to the ideals of personal autonomy conventionally associated with business proprietorship remain reluctantly attached to their jobs.

In this chapter, we have discussed a number of ways in which managerial careers are changing. In particular, we have described how managers, faced with considerable job uncertainties, are reassessing the importance of career pursuit and the extent to which their employing organizations are able to fulfil their occupational expectations. Thus, in view of our discussions in this and the previous chapter, we would envisage the organizational commitment of managers, particularly at middle and junior levels, to be declining. Despite variations according to such factors as age, technical specialism and personal aspiration, the overall trend would seem to be in this direction. But how far are the experiences of men distinct from their female colleagues? More women are now appointed to middle and junior management positions and although we have discussed certain aspects of their experiences we have not, as yet, assessed the extent to which *gender* may have important effects. We now turn our attention to these.

Notes

1   Of course, we recognize that we are presenting a *model* which is general in its applicability but from which there were variations according to such factors as organizational size, industrial sector and type of technology.
2   Deferred gratification has frequently been seen as an integral dimension of middle-class value systems (Parkin, 1971).
3   Often by 'selling back' services and professional skills to their previous employers.
4   Hence, the growing importance of staff appraisal schemes and assessment centres as mechanisms for determining the suitability of junior colleagues for promotion.
5   The present-day importance which senior managers attach to corporate cultures is an expression of this.
6   This both affects and reaffirms the process of polarization which is occurring within management. The expansion of graduate training in business administration in Britain over the past twenty years is an expression of this trend.
7   This is in sharp contrast to the experience of 'highly successful' managers who refuse to contemplate retirement and thus, when forced to give up work, experience considerable problems of psychological adjustment.

CHAPTER 5

Women, work and careers

Studies of corporate managers tend to assume that they are men (Rothwell, 1985). Accordingly, most of what we know about career expectations, job satisfactions and 'life priorities' is derived from the observation of their experiences (Marshall, 1984). In the 1950s and 1960s such a bias was understandable given the overwhelming dominance of men within managerial positions. In the 1980s, however, such an emphasis is unacceptable in view of the increasing number of women who are now employed in management (Nicholson and West, 1988). In this book, we have integrated their experiences within our general discussion even though this has often not been easy since women managers differ from their male colleagues in considerable ways. They tend to be younger, single and of middle-class origins.[1] They are more highly educated, but even so, they are less likely to be appointed to senior management positions. When they are working in comparable jobs to their male colleagues, they are usually paid less. But perhaps what is most significant is that the majority of women find themselves working in organizations that are dominated by *men* and this, both explicitly and implicitly, can operate to their disadvantage (Kanter, 1977). Nevertheless, their experiences do vary according to different work settings (Marshall, 1984). In this chapter we try to identify some of these and the ways in which they are associated with distinct personal and organizational circumstances.

Since women managers are primarily located in middle or junior positions they are particularly prone to experience pressures of the kind which we have discussed in previous chapters (Davidson and Cooper, 1983). Like their male colleagues they increasingly find themselves having to work longer hours with fewer resources, while often being subject to tighter controls and tougher performance measures.[2] They frequently have limited career prospects and some face the threat of redundancy as a consequence of corporate restructuring. Although, as we have already pointed out, they are usually more accustomed than men to insecurities in their careers, 82 per cent of those who took part in our survey feel they face 'greater pressures than men as managers'. These are associated with a variety of factors relating to their work and non-work experiences. While some encounter conflicting demands associated with work and its relationship with their personal lifestyles, others are confronted with solely occupation-based pressures. In particular, a significant proportion of them feel an exceptional need to achieve because of expectations which, they think, men have of them. Others find their corporate visibility as women managers together with their working relationships with male colleagues, subordinates and immediate bosses to be important sources of stress. In order to pursue these issues we asked the women in our survey to describe the major sources of their pressures. The coded responses are reported in Figure 5.1.

These feelings reflect a familiar pattern and are consistent with the findings of studies conducted both in Britain and the United States (Bartol, 1980; Cooper and Davidson, 1982; Davidson and Cooper, 1983; Hennig and Jardim, 1979). Most women managers, it seems, encounter demands which, they feel, do not affect men. 'Whether married or single', comments one respondent, 'a woman manager usually has the additional pressure of looking after a home. Few men realize what effect this has' (female, late 40s, General Management). She refers, like many others in our survey, to the tensions involved in balancing work-related demands with domestic roles. At the same time, she is implying that these are not solely confined to *married* women.[3] Those who are

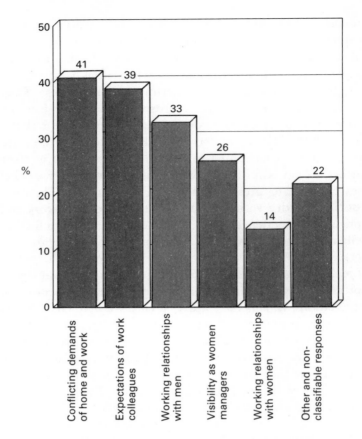

Figure 5.1 Major pressures reported by women managers.

single, like unmarried men, do not have the domestic support of partners. *Unlike* single men, however, such women are often confronted with demands to care for elderly parents and other dependent relatives, particularly if they are the 'only' daughters. Indeed, women managers who are married are able to avoid such commitments because of their own family responsibilities which, if carefully managed, can enable them to cope better than their single counterparts with potential conflicts between their careers and home lives. Even very

[108]

limited domestic support from their partners may be preferable, after all, to no support at all.

Such contrasts are particularly pronounced between *older* single women and their *younger* married female colleagues. The former tend to describe their earlier work experiences as a series of relatively unrelated 'jobs' such that only after some years do they identify particular patterns of progress which can be recognized as constituting careers. It is only then that they realize that such careers have implications for their personal lives. In many ways, as members of a 'first generation' of female corporate managers, they became aware of these personal costs when, according to many of them, it was too late. As a middle manager in her late 40s, now living with her widowed mother, says:

> When I joined the organization in 1953, it was just a job as far as I was concerned . . . It was only when I joined this particular office some time afterwards, that I began to look at it as a career. I suppose it was a mixture of things. I perhaps became more confident in myself and began to realize that a woman *could* make a career in this organization and do well . . . My father was a manual worker and I came from a very ordinary working–class family. I have managed to better myself, unexpectedly perhaps, from a very rough beginning. The things I've achieved have been very satisfying . . . It so happened that I haven't married. That again was not a direct choice. It's just the way the cookie crumbled, if you like, given the way my career developed . . . But, although I'm single, I've got – in a way – a dependent and this is one of the points I argue with men, of course. I feel I've got a greater responsibility than they have now. I mean as a person gets older – even though my mother would still like to feel independent – they do get dependent upon you. Whereas, of course, a husband and wife team, they're both much of the same age and if they're both out earning then, great stuff, you know! (female, late 40s, Personnel).

Not surprisingly, she offers the following advice to younger women:

> Try to look at yourself and make a decision on which way you

want to go. Make your aims quite clear and set your targets. That's what I'd be saying to a young person. I wouldn't put my example up as a good one because much of it has happened, certainly in the early years, purely by chance. And all because when I left school, I knew I was going to have to go out and work – and it was just work. I was very naive. When I look back on it, I just accepted what I was asked to do. (female, late 40s, Personnel).

In the light of their older female colleagues' experiences, better educated women are more likely to develop explicit personal career strategies. As such, they anticipate the possible conflicts which may occur if they attempt simultaneously to fulfil different work and non-work ambitions. Accordingly, they are forced to make choices about appropriate potential partners, jobs, careers and even residential locations (Marshall, 1984). Many feel their career chances are improved with a carefully 'screened' and 'selected' partner rather than if they choose to remain single. As a woman in her 20s describes her personal circumstances:

I really don't think I'd have been as successful if I hadn't been married – or married to someone that didn't understand. You see, I think the ideal compromise is to have the backing of a husband. Two of you sharing the hassle and someone supporting you. I can understand why it's difficult for lots of women to succeed because they're playing a submissive role. But there *is* an option. You should really interview my husband because he's rare – he has a more equal attitude than any other man I've come across. I'm convinced that's the best basis. I know from my early career days when I was single, that I was less effective – even accounting for age and experience – than I am now. (female, late 40s, Personnel).

In their attempts to secure an appropriate balance between career-related demands and domestic responsibilities, then, women managers tend to face different problems to their male colleagues. This is especially the case for those with children and it is often parenthood rather than marriage that would seem to be more significant in generating home–work conflicts (Gutek, Nakamura and Nieva, 1981; Larwood and Wood, 1977). This is hardly surprising given the pressures for men and women managers to work *longer* hours and within employment structures which do not permit, without disadvantage, work interruptions associated with child rearing.[4] The irony, of course, is that many women choose to forego parenthood in pursuit of their careers, only to find that they continue to suffer their male colleagues' suspicions that they *might,* at some time in the future, restructure their personal priorities (Rothwell, 1985).

But what of other sources of pressure which derive specifically from women's relationships with their male colleagues? As Figure 5.1 suggests, 39 per cent of women managers feel the need to meet the expectations of men while 25 per cent refer to pressures relating to their corporate visibility. These two factors are, of course, closely interrelated. As Kanter (1977) has argued, in situations where men are numerically and politically dominant – as they are in most work organizations – women are usually viewed as 'tokens' and as such are subject to three 'perceptual tendencies': those associated with *visibility, contrast* and *assimilation.* She argues:

> First, tokens get attention. One by one, they have higher *visibility* than dominants looked at alone; they capture a larger awareness share . . . *Contrast* or polarization and exaggeration of differences – is the second perceptual tendency. In uniform groups, members and observers may never become self-conscious about the common culture and type, which remain taken for granted and implicit. But the presence of a person or two bearing a different set of social characteristics increases the self-consciousness of the numerically dominant population . . . *Assimilation,* the third perceptual tendency, involves the use of stereotypes, or familiar generalizations about a person's social type. The characteristics of a token tend to be distorted to fit the generalization. Tokens are more easily stereotyped than people found in greater proportion. (pp.210–11; our italics).

[111]

Each of these perceptions generates characteristic responses. Thus, *visibility* creates 'pressures to perform'. Indeed, many of the women in our survey are acutely aware of such demands and the following are representative of the comments included in our questionnaire:

> The constant need to prove oneself. (female, late 40s, Research and Development).

> Having to be better than a man to be perceived the same. (female, late 40s, Personnel).

> Needing to be infallible. (female, late 20s, Sales and Marketing).

> Being considered by most men as second-class citizens unable to do the job as well as they do. (female, late 30s, General Management).

Such tensions stem from a variety of sources. As we argued in Chapter 4, because some women are perceived by their male colleagues almost as 'strangers' or even as 'trespassers' and, hence, not entirely trustworthy, they feel compelled to demonstrate their competence through more explicit and measurable performance criteria. Indeed, they can feel obliged to overachieve in order to refute many of the prevailing stereotypical assumptions which they perceive are generally held by men (Davidson and Cooper, 1983). Further, because they constitute a minority of all managers, *individual* women experience great pressures to produce outstanding results since they are aware that their male colleagues regard them as 'representatives' of *all* women. In this sense, women managers feel that they are setting precedents which will influence the extent to which their junior female colleagues are regarded as competent successors. Even those who are able to avoid the more extreme outcomes of 'visibility' in their immediate, day-to-day working relationships remain aware that, within broader organizational

[112]

contexts, they may be regarded as token representatives. As one remarks:

> The people that work closest to you treat you as an individual manager. But the more distanced you get, either up or down the organization or outside in social life, then the more you're seen very much as 'a woman'. . . you're back to the old stereotypes . . . Even those around you don't entirely forget you're a woman. Really it's a difference that's recognized in much the same way as a coloured senior manager is recognized for the fact that he's black. They're unique. There aren't many around. And youth, the younger you are, the more you're regarded as unique. Our new chairman is young and it comes out every time someone comments on him . . . it's the unique features that influence how they interpret his actions. I put women in the same category. While we are in a minority, we will be initially viewed as women and interpreted in that way until people begin to recognize that there's not very much difference. (female, late 20s, Personnel).

Just as *visibility* generates among women managers feelings that they need to demonstrate their competence, so gender-related *contrasts* or differences reinforce the boundaries which tend to exist between men and women in most large-scale organizations. The very existence of women as tokens can reaffirm the common bonds and affinities that men enjoy and sustain the extent to which their female managerial colleagues are perceived as 'outsiders' (Marshall, 1984). Indeed, their presence may be discomforting since it can lead men to rethink many of the dominant assumptions and premises which are steeped in male-based forms of control. As a result, women managers may be perceived as a threat to existing managerial practices. 'The males gang up on you', says a women in our study, 'and they treat you as though you are trespassing on their preserve. You are not treated as a woman, you are treated as an intruder' (female, early 50s, Personnel). Indeed, men can exclude their female colleagues from personal networks and informal communication systems by, for example, talking endlessly about (male) sports and by relating various sexist stories and jokes. As such, male-based cultures are sustained within managerial hierarchies and these serve to uphold the dominant position of men and effectively reinforce the barriers which women face in their career ambitions. They are, then, forced to make a fundamental decision: either to accept and adhere to these values or attempt to reject them (Goffee and Scase, 1985). If the latter, they are likely to be perceived by their male colleagues as 'odd' and to be further excluded from various informal but, nevertheless, important interpersonal networks. If, on the other hand, they accept the predominant assumptions, they are likely to enhance their own career prospects but to the disadvantage of women in general (Cooper and Davidson, 1982). Usually the former strategy represents the most convenient means of overcoming threats of personal exclusion. As one of them explains:

> Some fellas I've worked with didn't think there should be a woman working with them . . . But fortunately most that I've worked with have become friendly and treated me as one of them. But I'm not a woman at work, I'm treated as a man, definitely. It doesn't bother me – I'd rather be like that. I mean, we all go out to the pub and there's no 'Oh, pull out the chair for Jane' or only buy her a drink, she's not allowed to buy you one. We all take it in turns on rounds. The only criterion they laid down was that I had to drink pints! And I learnt very quickly that you had to *hold* them as well – not slur when you've had one! They treat me as a man, basically – I'm one of the boys . . . I've got to take it as read that if I'm in the company of men the language that they use is pretty choice. You either muck in or – it's no good turning round and saying, 'I'm sorry, I don't want you talking like that'. . . At our Wednesday meetings at work, I'm the only woman and my boss gets fed up of saying 'Lady and Gentlemen', so it's 'I know you don't mind, Jane, I'll just call you one of the boys'. . . It's always going to be a man's world . . . it's never going to be any different because there are never going to be enough women. The majority are always going to want children – that's the pattern of life over the centuries. So, on that basis, you've got to work with them and know how they

[114]

work . . . Separate training is of no relevance whatsoever – because, again, you've got wet women as much as you've got wet blokes . . . But in our office, it's a standard joke that I'm a tougher nut to crack than any of the men . . . They think I'm a very hard woman. (female, late 30s, Finance and Accounting).

However, other women may be assimilated into one of a number of different negative stereotypes (Davidson and Cooper, 1983). In this process, women are allocated to various roles which underplay their managerial skills and technical competences but which reinforce more traditional, gender-related attributes. Many women complain, for example, that despite their formal managerial positions, they are often perceived and treated as 'secretaries' and 'assistants'. Others find themselves stereotyped as corporate 'wives' who offer care and affection or 'mothers' who are expected to be sympathetic and understanding. As such, they can find themselves forced into various counsellor roles, with their male colleagues expecting them to be selflessly concerned with resolving other people's problems. In this process their own managerial status and identity tends to become marginalized. Yet others, however, can be cast into the roles of 'girls' and, as such, any attempts by them to be independent and assertive can be severely undermined. They cease to be perceived as threatening to the male-based dominant corporate order and their achievements are patronizingly recognized in terms of what Kanter (1977) aptly sums up as a 'kind of look-what-she-did-and-she's-only-a-woman attitude' (p.235). Perhaps more than any other stereotype, it is this identity which denies that women can ever be taken seriously as managers and this, particularly, sustains the patriarchal nature of most large-scale organizations (Oakley, 1982). Of course, some women may be personally accepted by male colleagues because of their physical attractiveness rather than as a result of their managerial competences. Indeed, there are usually strong pressures for them to conform to predominant male ideas about 'appearance', 'attraction' and 'charm', since failure to do so can lead them to be negatively assessed as 'feminists'. As such, they can be even more marginalized within different corporate settings and their promotion and career prospects further undermined.

How do women cope with these tendencies? Some become excessively formal and impersonal in their manner of speech, their interactions with others and their style of dress in order to reaffirm the responsibility of their positions and their managerial identities. Others play the stereotypical role to which they have been allocated and make the best of things. Thus, they will deliberately exploit 'female' attributes in order to enhance their careers. Those seen as 'girls' can use their physical attraction as a means of personal influence with their senior male colleagues. Similarly, 'mothers' can use the confidential information which they obtain from their colleagues for their own ends. Some women try to reduce their personal 'visibility', through dress, manners and presentation of self. By adopting a non-assertive identity they are able to blend more easily into the dominant male culture and, thereby, avoid many of the tendencies forcing them into roles of the sort we have discussed above. Such a tactic can enable them to improve their career prospects but, at the same time, there can be risks that their various personal achievements will not be fully recognized (Kanter, 1977). Many of the older women in our study favour this strategy although they complain that it can lead to their efforts being 'taken for granted'.

However, some women are managers in work settings where patriarchy is less pronounced. This is more often the case in those organizations where there are higher proportions of women in senior managerial positions. In our study, for example, women employed by the leisure services corporation feel they are subject to fewer pressures associated with 'tokenism'. As one remarks:

> I found far less stress when I joined this company because there are so many more of us . . . You didn't feel the same

pressures. There was an established acceptance of women in fairly high-level jobs . . . Equal weight is given to men and women. This happens a great deal more than in other industries because it's an acceptable job for a women . . . Instinctively, I felt that food and catering were more receptive to women than other industries. I mean, I think that engineering would be much more difficult to get beyond a very low level. (female, early 50s, Personnel).

Of course, many occupations, industries and organizations have become gender-stereotyped due to the overwhelming predominance of women as employees (Wainright, 1984; Webb, 1982; West, 1982). Typically this has been the case in some 'service' and 'caring' sectors where salaries and status rewards are low (Goffee and Scase, 1985). Even so, some women prefer to be managers within organizations where equal opportunities legislation is taken seriously and where there is some attempt to enforce meritocratic criteria of selection and promotion. This could explain why there are more women in middle and senior management positions in public rather than in private sector corporations (Alban-Metcalfe and Nicholson, 1984; Rothwell, 1985). One woman manager compares her experiences as follows:

I don't think I've encountered discrimination directly in this organization. When I first worked it was understood that you weren't in a career, you know, you were filling in time. *That* was discrimination because it's saying that you're not in a career. But all that did was encourage me to move around until I found somewhere that *did* offer a career. And I've found that attitude here . . . Of course, you've got to show you're interested, but, once you've given yourself the initial kick and said, 'Look what I can do', they say, 'Well, look at these courses.' Once you've qualified, you can do this. You can raise your head above the crowd. That's the difference. (female, early 30s, Administration).

However, there are other work settings, in both public and private sectors, where the complex nature of the tasks in hand

[117]

requires such a high level of technical expertise that gender-related attributes are regarded as less important. In many of the new and rapidly expanding occupations in such areas as computing, advertising, public relations and consultancy, women are more likely to be regarded as professional colleagues rather than as members of a secondary or subordinate group. As two of them working in such areas explain:

> I've always felt that once you've established yourself, people realize you know what you're talking about. That you're of above average intelligence and you're not going to burst into tears every time someone shouts at you; that you can stand on your own feet. Then people recognize you for the job that you're doing . . . I've never really had any trouble . . . some guys were a bit suspicious and a bit wary at first . . . but once you've proved to them you're there because you genuinely can do it, then they accept you. I really don't feel being a woman makes much difference . . . Personally, I don't care if it's a man or a woman in the team. All I care about is their ability to do the job, their attitude and their maturity . . . people good at man management, people who are technically brilliant – you need a good mix. (female, late 20s, Computing).

> I don't think any of us go around thinking, 'I'm a female manager'. . . Once you're making people accept you as you are . . . When it comes to the crunch, you can either do it or you can't and people accept you on that basis – whether you're male or female, got two heads or whatever . . . In a computer department, women are not unusual . . . If I've had problems, it's not because I'm female . . . I've three older men who've been team leaders in their environment working for me now . . . they've been wonderful, very supportive. You treat them as equals. We've all got a role to play in this project. My role is to put it all together – men and women. (female, late 30s, Management Services).

Thus, there are work situations were women do not feel threatened or undermined by their male colleagues; the latter may be keen to act as mentors, offering advice and support to female subordinates in order to help them in their careers (Clutterbuck and Devine, 1987; Hennig and Jardim, 1979). Similarly there may be circumstances where women are less likely to be excluded from informal networks. This can occur when there are tightly knit task-oriented work teams consisting of those with particular technical competences – for example, engineers, scientists, and specialists of one kind or another – who carve out 'communities at work'. In such contexts, men and women colleagues 'talk shop' and informal relationships can reinforce effective operating performance. But for women in more traditional, 'male dominated' organizations where informal networks are more readily distinguishable from formally prescribed work tasks, there can be difficulties (Goffee and Scase, 1986). Attempts to break into such networks may serve only to reinforce existing stereotypes. One woman manager describes her experience as follows:

> I try to work in a close relationship with men and always have done . . . it's often all men and me . . . On one job, I was with the chief of security all day and, of course, I was 'having a mad passionate affair with him'. That went around the office for the next fifteen months . . . I'm the type of person that doesn't just want to have a working relationship. Let's talk about the family and everything else . . . Let's go for a drink at lunchtime – you know, great! Of course, it causes gossip . . . I come home to my husband and say, 'Guess who I'm having an affair with this week.' (female, late 30s, Finance and Accounting).

If women, generally, have difficulties in their relationships with their immediate bosses and colleagues so, too, can they face problems in managing both their male and female subordinates. As one of the respondents says, 'Although generalizations are risky, the average male resents being "bossed" by a female, while the average female resents a female boss as being an upstart' (female, early 30s, Engineering and Development). Such attitudes could be changing. A

[119]

recent survey, for example, suggests that nine out of ten European male managers feel that women can perform their managerial tasks just as well as their male counterparts (Rothwell, 1985). However, their credibility often remains low. This would seem to be, at least partially, a function of the discrepancy that exists between their identities as *women* and as *managers*. As one of them states:

> Where women are managing men, it's difficult. It's just the way society is structured. You have the problem of what sort of relationship you are going to establish. For example, a man will go off and take a subordinate to the pub and sort things out over a pint. I don't use that sort of style myself. I think it's more difficult for a woman to establish the right relationships that doesn't make the man feel crushed. (female, early 50s, Personnel).

Such dilemmas are inevitably linked to prevailing 'fashions' about effective managerial styles. As we discussed in Chapter 3, more assertive interpersonal skills are now more highly valued. Consequently, the pressures facing women managers may be increasing as they feel encouraged to be more 'directive' and 'autocratic'. Indeed, 88 per cent of those in our survey refer to the need to be 'tough', 'aggressive', 'firm' and 'assertive', while less than 50 per cent mention the desirability of a more 'open', 'co-operative' and 'consultative' approach. This preference is particularly evident among the younger respondents, three of whom describe their notions of effectiveness in the following terms:

> I find I get the best results by being firm about what I want and fair about the results. I don't think playing the 'helpless female' works any more; you'd get stamped on these days. But giving your personnel the opportunity to say what they think about the situation in general is a useful guide as to how to correct or improve things which go astray. Timescales are always a problem, but, by ensuring they know what's expected by when and why in the first place, their enthusiasm can be maintained. (female, late 30s, Engineering and Development).

[120]

Be firm and decisive at all times. Communicate well with superiors, colleagues and subordinates. Be fair. Do not make reference to being a woman . . . Look for areas of improvement and always be critical of yourself and the current methods of doing things. Always aim to improve profits and productivity. Listen to the people who work for you. (female, late 20s, Engineering and Development).

Independent thought, coupled with an adult style, which does not aggressively appear masculine. An ability to make sound decisions, manage firmly, be firm and 'better' than male colleagues. Open, competitive, independent, leading from the front, non-autocratic and, above all, attentive. (female, early 50s, Personnel).

However, there are those who feel that their gender gives them as *women* particular qualities which can be useful in their managerial roles (Goffee and Scase, 1985; LaRouche and Ryan, 1984). Hence, they often refer to a distinctively female style of leadership which emphasizes care, informality and a personal concern for the individual. Some examples of such views, as expressed on our questionnaire, are as follows:

I think the most effective style of leadership for women managers is one which encourages staff to work together . . . I find that as a woman manager working largely with men it's difficult not to slip into a fairly masculine role when dealing with staff. I have to make a conscious effort to try and encourage the individual to develop him or herself. But this is where women managers have a key role to play in bringing balance to effective leadership – especially in large, male dominated organizations. (female, early 30s, Finance and Accounting).

I think women need to adopt a rather informal style; there's nothing more ridiculous than a shrill, angry woman! Laughter and gentle mockery are usually far more effective than anger. This leads to a gentle, informal style where approval, cajolery and mockery replace approval, orders and anger, respectively. It is absolutely necessary to get your facts right, be accurate and quick on your feet though to gain respect as this style does

[121]

not invoke respect through fear. (female, early 30s, Engineering and Development).

They should adopt a style which allows flexibility from their subordinates – a chance for people to input new ideas which the manager can co-ordinate. Women, I feel, are 'open' in their approach and can, therefore, get more out of employees than their male colleagues. (female, late 20s, Personnel).

A very sensitive approach is needed with a high degree of 'sociability' – but a logical and forceful approach on strategy, planning, etc. I do not believe women can survive with an autocratic leader – Mrs Thatcher is an exception. An influential, persuasive and consultative approach is more relevant. (female, late 20s, Personnel).

It is important for a woman to consult and involve her own team to gain commitment. In addition, she must be well respected by her subordinates and colleagues and make high personal standards. In one word, she should be democratic. (female, late 40s, General Management).

These women, then, are adhering to 'people-centred' styles at a time when senior managers in many corporations are often encouraging more assertive and task-centred approaches.[6] Unless they work in corporate settings where these 'softer' styles are valued, such as in 'creative', welfare and high-technology organizations, they run the risk of being considered as possessing inappropriate qualities for promotion to senior management positions. This may explain why, despite their increasing numbers at middle managerial levels, fewer women are reaching higher corporate positions today than in the 1970s (Van de Vliet, 1988). In this sense, therefore, the barriers which they face in their careers may be increasing rather than declining.

What, then, are the implications for their motivation and commitment? Will the growing numbers of well-qualified women with high work aspirations make even greater efforts to achieve in male-dominated organizations, or will they simply reduce their aspirations and be satisfied with middle-level management jobs? A recent study suggests that women managers exhibit 'considerable dynamism to overcome the odds against them. They achieve equivalent status to the men by being better qualified, more ambitious and more mobile' (Alban-Metcalfe and Nicholson, 1984, p.41). Indeed, this investigation argues that while male managers assess themselves as *less* ambitious at work, their female colleagues rate themselves as more ambitious in their jobs. Our own survey also suggests differences in their work orientations. As we reported in Chapter 4, whereas only 18 per cent of male managers rank career achievements as the most important source of satisfaction in their lives, this was the case for no fewer than 30 per cent of the women. How, then, do these more *career-oriented women* differ from other women taking part in our survey? Certainly, our data suggest that they are more successful. Two-thirds of them earn more than £15,000 per annum compared with less than 40 per cent of the entire group of women managers in the study. Perhaps, surprisingly, they are more likely to be married or living with a partner – 73 per cent compared with an overall figure of 55 per cent. This does seem to confirm our earlier suggestion that for women managers, marriage, *in itself,* is not an obstacle in their careers and does not necessarily reflect a change in their attitudes towards work or, even, priorities in life. Given partners who are sympathetic to the demands of their careers and who are prepared to defer parenthood, it is possible for women managers to continue to regard their jobs as central within their life interests. In this sense, therefore, marriage or domestic relationships may become *grafted upon* already-established life priorities and occupational commitments. One of these career-oriented married woman describes her attitude as follows:

> I see it as a career rather than just a job. I made a conscious decision for a career a long time ago . . . I've tried to be fairly general rather than specialist – too many women get trapped

[123]

as specialists . . . I decided I would go and do whatever was considered necessary to get me where I wanted to go . . . The way I see it, you have to make a choice in life to pursue a career and stick at it. I feel that women who break off and have families, they're the ones who get discriminated against . . . they become pregnant and they're written off – wiped out . . . I haven't got that problem . . . I've got no maternal feelings and never have had – so there's not that conflict between my domestic and business life. (female, late 40s, Research and Development).

Thus, it appears that *both* married and single women can, in appropriate work and domestic circumstances, obtain levels of satisfaction from their jobs which are comparable with those enjoyed by men. It is, or course, questionable whether this will continue if their opportunities for promotion into senior positions remain highly restricted. However, most of those in our own study are optimistic about trends as these are affecting the opportunities available in management for women *in general*. Indeed, when asked 'How do you see career patterns emerging for women managers in the long-term future?', more than half of them predict a decline in discrimination, as shown in Figure 5.2.

Two women explain the reasons for their optimism in the following terms:

I believe there is now a greater awareness of the need to provide women with greater opportunities for career development. There is less prejudice against women than before. My own experience suggests a genuine desire to appoint to a managerial post the best candidate, irrespective of their sex. Provided women respond to the challenge – by seeking appropriate qualifications and experience to compete on equal terms with their male counterparts, then the trend appears to be that careers will be given every opportunity to blossom. (female, late 30s, Administration).

I think there will be a slow but definite move towards more flexible career patterns to reflect the growing awareness that women do not fit easily into a career structure designed for the

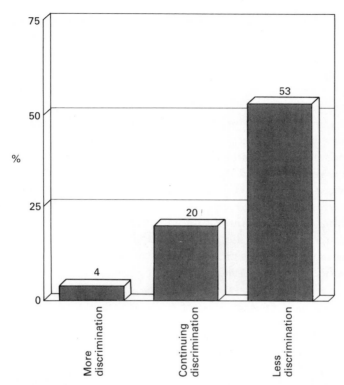

Figure 5.2 Perceived career opportunities for women managers in the future.

traditional working man. This will be aided by the increasing levels of organizational instability which are affecting male career patterns. (female, early 30s, Personnel).

Some, however, are more pessimistic. One of them, for example, makes the following observation:

A lot depends on economic and social conditions. A hard economic climate makes it more difficult for women to succeed. I do not foresee any radical changes in traditionally male dominated organizations. Any progress is likely to be slow with few women reaching top management positions except in areas which are regarded as traditionally female. (female, early 50s, Personnel).

[125]

But irrespective of the ways in which they see *general* future trends, ambitious women managers face a variety of frustrations in their *particular* jobs and encounter a number of career barriers. It is in response to these that more of them are opting out of corporate careers and deciding to start their own businesses (Goffee and Scase, 1985). Indeed, as we have already reported, more than half of those co-operating in our study have contemplated start-up in the hope that entrepreneurship can offer them new opportunities. In starting such ventures they often use the technical skills which they have acquired in their jobs, particularly when they are in such areas as market research, advertising, public relations, publishing, software computing and management consultancy.[8] Their motives are aptly summarized in the following comments of two entrepreneurs interviewed in an earlier study (Goffee and Scase, 1985):

> I'm quite ambitious. I want to do various things with my life . . . But, in my last job, there was no future in it. I set up this business because I was fed up with people saying, 'Are you thinking of getting married?' or, 'Are you having a child?' I got sick to death of it. Never got anywhere. Well, I thought, I don't have to put up with this. Who needs to? If you set up something on your own, as long as you survive, you don't have to listen to that. I love not having all those office politics. I just get on with my work. (female, early 30s, Proprietor).

> After I got married, I announced to the Board that I was going to have a baby . . . They refused to accept that I wanted to come back as managing director of their subsidiary. They brought in somebody over me and demoted me to director, even though I was back at work after two months . . . They would not accept that you can be a managing director as well as a working mother. This resistance and totally stupid attitude meant an important turning point for me. I felt desperately I could do better . . . just as simple as that. I got fed up with being employed. I wanted to be an employer . . . I wanted autonomy, to be able to run my own business. (female, early 50s, Proprietor).

Women managers who start their own businesses, then, do not necessarily reject the success goals or values of the occupational order. On the contrary, they regard entrepreneurship as an alternative route for achieving these; a means whereby personal effort and ability can be better rewarded. Female entrepreneurs, rather like many women managers, are usually highly committed to their work, but they tend to differ from many of their corporate colleagues in seeking greater rewards in terms of pay, job satisfaction, personal development and responsibilities. They regard entrepreneurship as a means of escaping from the middle echelons of large corporations where they often feel 'trapped' because of male-based assumptions which can limit their opportunities.

To conclude, despite the increasing numbers of women who are being appointed to middle and junior managerial positions, their experiences of work are often quite different from those of their male colleagues. As we have shown, these can vary according to a number of factors such as age, marital status and organizational setting. Younger women, in particular, may often select work environments where gender-based prejudices are less pronounced. But it is debatable whether this will enable many of them to gain access to senior positions, given the nature of present-day corporate assumptions about the desirability of assertive management styles. It is, then, hardly surprising that some of them decide to leave large-scale organizations to start their own businesses. Most, however, remain – for a time, at least – and in the next chapter we turn our attention to the ways in which they and their male colleagues develop lifestyles and personal relationships outside work.

Notes

1   This, of course, is partly a reflection of the increasing participation of women in institutions of higher education during the 1960s and 1970s.

2 As we discussed in Chapter 2.

3 We use the term 'married' to refer to all of those respondents living with partners, irrespective of registered legal status.

4 There are striking contrasts between employing organizations in their policies towards this matter. We suspect, however, that in general, those in public sector are rather more generous than others.

5 Unfortunately, there is a lack of evidence on behaviour within organizations in which women occupy the majority of management positions. There are, of course, few such instances. However, some of the larger businesses set up and managed by women offer research opportunities for investigating the extent to which distinctive 'female' styles of leadership may become prevalent within organizational settings.

6 This trend is reflected in the present-day popularity of 'business heroes' whose published autobiographies now sell millions of copies worldwide and which often become serialized in newspapers and popular magazines.

7 Many of our respondents were ultimately pessimistic about their own personal career opportunities, but optimistic for the longer term possibilities for women *in general*.

8 Such business ventures often require little capital funding and accordingly start-up is that much easier.

CHAPTER 6

Home lives and personal lifestyles

So far in this book we have focused upon the behaviour of managers *within* organizations; that is, in terms of their jobs, their relationships with others and their careers. In this chapter we turn our attention to aspects of their personal lives and, in particular, consider the extent to which these are affected by their experiences at work. Obviously jobs do have an important impact upon lifestyles since these determine not only living standards, but also the time constraints of leisure and home life, as well as personal status and identity. It is for such reasons that unemployment or redundancy can have traumatic repercussions and go far beyond those hardships that are simply associated with loss of earnings (Fineman, 1983; Wood, 1980). However, although the nature of their jobs can have pervading effects for managers' personal identities and lifestyles, there are considerable variations in the extent and nature of these. While some are able to 'switch off' and maintain sharp boundaries between work and leisure, others cannot. Sometimes, there will be work-related crises which will psychologically invade 'free time', while in other circumstances managers will feel able to relax outside their normal working hours. Thus, the boundaries separating work and leisure are often ambiguous since psychological preoccupations with work can often spill over into 'free' time (Evans and Bartolomé, 1980).

The relationship between work and 'non-work' has long been an interest of social scientists (Parker, 1983). Indeed, many of the themes explored by early observers were concerned with the ways in which employment within large-scale organizations shapes other aspects of non-work behaviour. According to some writers the experience of employment is inevitably alienating and impoverishes all other aspects of life.[1] Thus, only work which occurs *outside* employment relationships offers the possibilities for self-expression and personal fulfilment (Gorz, 1982). Others argue that the more impersonal features of modern social life have been largely caused by the growth of large-scale industrial organizations and their excessive division of work tasks (Braverman, 1974). According to this view, employment can be enriched and personal satisfaction enhanced if more broadly-defined and *flexible* work roles are created.[2] Although, therefore, there are often differences in the extent to which the possibility of psychologically rewarding employment is conceded – given the nature of modern large-scale organizations – its overriding significance for shaping personal identities and life experiences is almost universally agreed.

As a result of such concerns, a large body of material has developed which describes the influence of work experiences on family relationships, leisure activities and more general lifestyles. For managers, in particular, there have been studies of the ways in which their jobs affect the nature of family systems (Bott, 1957; Young and Willmot, 1973), conjugal roles (Bell, 1968; Edgell, 1980; Rapaport and Rapaport, 1976) and the domestic division of labour (Pahl and Pahl, 1971; Handy, 1978). Similarly, there have been investigations of leisure activities (Evans and Bartolomé, 1980; Pahl and Pahl, 1971; Parker, 1983) and explorations of the identity-conferring properties of managerial occupations (Sofer, 1970; Hunt and Collins, 1983). But despite the accumulation of such data there remains considerable limitations in our understanding of the relationships that exist between the work and non-work experiences of managers. First, many analyses exhibit forms of one-way determinism in assuming that the nature of work or employment shapes *all* other aspects of

[130]

personal and social experience (Evans and Bartolomé, 1980). Rarely, therefore, is the reverse possibility considered whereby non-work factors, such as family and social class background, locality, education and so on, can affect behaviour at work. Thus, most studies assume that for male managers, at least, factors beyond the workplace are relatively unimportant, except perhaps in times of personal crisis. This is in sharp contrast to the treatment of women who, it is assumed, can be preoccupied with personal, family and domestic responsibilities which may 'spill over' into work (Rapaport and Rapaport, 1976). Consequently, it is often argued that many women managers lack the commitment to pursue careers in the same fashion as their male colleagues. This, in turn, highlights a second inadequacy in the literature on the possible links between work and non-work; much of the data is derived from the experiences of men. Given the increase in the proportion of women entering managerial and professional occupations, the interplay between their experiences of work, family and leisure needs to be more fully explored; so far, it is mainly working-class women who have been the focus of attention (Pahl, 1984). Such studies highlight a third limitation; generally, investigations of work or employment experiences are (falsely) separated from the analysis of leisure patterns. As one observer has pointed out, leisure can be distinguished from work in terms of *time, activity, purpose,* and even in terms of *context* (Parker, 1971; 1986). Generally it is agreed that it refers to time or activities over which individuals can exercise a considerable degree of personal choice; they can choose what to do, when and where, according to their own personal preferences.

But there can be ambiguities in distinguishing the work and non-work roles of managers. Although they may be apparently 'relaxing' at home they may still be psychologically 'at work'. Managers in similar jobs may differ in their psychological commitment to work and leisure. Some are able to 'switch off' and keep a sharp distinction between their work and non-work lives while others seem unable to

[131]

preserve such boundaries. For some, any such distinction between work and leisure is meaningless simply because work *is* their lives. Even those who make conscious and sustained attempts to keep their leisure activities separate from work influences can find that crises in their jobs can psychologically invade their free time. For these reasons, then, it is difficult to establish precisely how far managers are able to carve out clearly defined spheres of personal autonomy during their non-work time.

A recent study of lifestyles among male managers distinguishes between five different patterns of relationship that exists between their work and non-work experiences (Evans and Bartolomé, 1980): (i) *spillover* – 'one affects the other, in a positive or negative way'; (ii) *independence* – 'they exist side by side and for all practical purposes are independent of each other'; (iii) *conflict* – 'they are in conflict with each other and cannot be easily reconciled'; (iv) *instrumentality* – 'one is primarily a means of obtaining something derived in the other'; and (v) *compensation* – 'one is a way of making up for what is missing in the other' (p.28). These patterns are associated with different work and career orientations which can be described as follows:

> The spillover relationship predominates where the manager is struggling to be successful. The independent relationship is one of equilibrium, where he is satisfied with his career progress. He feels confident in his abilities and has a sense of inner success. As evaluated by traditional work satisfaction measures, he is not likely to be more satisfied than his colleague who experiences spillover – the difference is that his professional life is free of the distress that is created by struggling. The conflict relationship develops where the manager feels highly satisfied and successful in his career, which feeds his sense of self-esteem. He too leads a professional life of high tension, but one characterised by stimulation and excitement rather than by the stress of insecurity and anxiety. Locked into a professional ego trip, his psychological involvement is directed almost exclusively to his career. This contrasts with the instrumental manager whose sense of career

[132]

failure has led to his gradual disengagement from his work.
(Evans and Bartolomé, 1980, p.36).

Despite such variations, the authors report that among those they studied the experience of *spillover* – possibly in conjunction with any one other pattern – is the most common relationship. But as they point out, 'professional and private lives are not inter-related reciprocally. The influence is one-way. It is the feelings generated by work that determine the quality of the relationship, and not the reverse' (p.39). The determining influence of work is further confirmed in their assessment that 'the most powerful influence in private life is the influence of negative feelings aroused at work' (p.16) and 'for managers at least a healthy professional life is a precondition for a well-functioning private life' (p.38).

To a considerable extent, we feel such conclusions are partly a function of the nature of the investigators' sample, consisting as it did of relatively successful male managers attending a leading European business school. Certainly this is not the overriding pattern in our own study; managers appear more likely to display work–leisure patterns characterized by *separation* and *instrumentality* rather than by 'one-way' *spillover*. This is not to deny, of course, that managers' jobs continue to influence their wider lifestyles to the extent that they broadly determine the time available for enjoying leisure and associated personal and home pursuits. Indeed, work experience can have important effects upon their personal identities. As some state, organizational constraints force them to behave in assertive, non-emotional and 'rational' ways and make it more difficult for them to be effective in their personal and family relationships. Those who are deeply involved in their jobs are at great risk of 'carrying over' their work-related identities into their private lives. Reluctant to 'role play' at work they are more likely to internalize occupationally-based criteria of personal conduct and so become 'hardened' (Hunt and Collins, 1983). They

[133]

and their partners often admit, on reflection, that work has made them, as managers, less 'caring', 'affectionate' and 'understanding' and more 'intolerant', 'cynical' and 'tough'. Changes of this kind are reflected in the following comments made by the men and women in our study:

> *Husband:* I think I've probably got less humour than I had . . . I think one tends to be rather more cynical and doubting about a great many things but I try not to let that come over when dealing with people. But, yes, I think I'm probably a little harsher and less tolerant towards people unless I try very hard. But I don't know, you've been around a long time, am I less amicable than I used to be?
> *Wife:* Yes. More intolerant of limitations, I suppose. You're bad tempered more often and it's all due to work, I'm sure, really. But you never used to be, twenty years ago. Nothing ever bothered you. You never got angry about anything, I don't think. You were the 'life and soul of the party' sort of character which you're not any longer, to be honest. (male, late 40s, General Management).

> I think there's a sort of toughness one has to develop which I think does rub off on to the other side of you life. I think we are under a great deal of self-control to put up with the pressures at work. So, I think that in your out-of-work life you're very controlled a lot of the time. But I think the other effect is that you do go off the deep end a lot and you can't do that at work. The wife gets a bit fed up with that. (male, early 40s, Production).

> I'm probably more abrupt. Instead of being a nice person, I can now be quite nasty because, you know, that's the way it is at work – it's a dog-eats-dog situation, isn't it? In business these days, anyway. There's no way you can take up a career and make friends at the same time – inside or outside work – if you do, it's by chance. (male, late 30s, Engineering).

> My wife gets the impression that most of the time I'm an out-and-out manager. I lay down the law. I tell people what they mustn't do and this, that and the other. And I'm the same at home as I am at work in relationships, you know. I go the

same way about it if I want Pam to do something for me. I go exactly the same way as at work, as if I was getting one of the fellas to do something for me. (male, early 50s, General Maintenance).

Women managers may feel under particular pressures to act in tough, assertive ways in their jobs. For them, as we have already pointed out, their careers can be particularly demanding because of the ways in which they are often forced to 'overachieve' in order to obtain senior positions within male-dominated organizations. Some feel, as we have shown, that to be successful they have to sacrifice many allegedly 'female' attributes such as 'sensitivity', 'consideration' and 'intuition' in order to develop more impersonal and less affective styles. Most of them are aware of work situations in which they need to play down their 'femininity' if they are to appear credible to their male colleagues and to avoid exclusion by them. Many, then, are keen to develop their assertiveness and self-confidence. As one claims:

As far as industry has treated me, I think I'm very lucky. I think I'm quite well balanced. But my bosses at work would say that I'm not very good at coping with the rough times. I think that's partly being a woman . . . I still need the experience and I'm still emotional. (female, late 20s, Personnel).

But the acquisition of such attributes, in order to be seen by male colleagues as 'effective', can have spillover effects for their behaviour outside work:

Sometimes, I come home from work and I still think I'm at work and I treat my husband like somebody at work. But, also, it's my attitude, it's by speaking more forcefully and sort of having more command in my presence. It's not something I choose but I do find it does exist. (female, early 20s, Personnel).

However, we must be careful not to overgeneralize from such personal experiences. As we discuss later in this chapter,

[135]

the spillover effects of workplace influences can be limited; certainly among women managers living with partners.

Of course, only some managers – male or female – are psychologically involved in their work. Career disappointments and the experience of being 'passed over' for promotion can lead them to distance themselves from their jobs and to perform only according to the minimum acceptable standards. In these cases senior managers will often become frustrated and impatient as their younger colleagues adjust to restricted career prospects by developing, over time, less intensive and more relaxed working practices. Evans and Bartolomé (1980) note this pattern when managers who, having experienced considerable spillover during the years when they were launching their careers, adopt more instrumental approaches to their jobs when they feel their future career prospects are severely curtailed. In our study, however, there are managers who appear to have *always* been unambitious and to have perceived their jobs in these terms. Accordingly, work seems to have little or no effect upon their personal identities, as the following comments illustrate:

> *Wife:* I don't think that it's work that has affected you. You've definitely matured, you know, but you would have done that whatever you'd been doing.
> *Husband:* Yes, I don't think I've changed very much. No. (male, early 50s, Finance and Accounting).

> I've never been an ambitious sort of character . . . I've never had another job. I came into this straight from school at 17 and I've been in it all my life apart from doing national service . . . I don't think I've changed . . . I've always been fairly easy going . . . possibly too easy going, but it just happens to be me. (male, late 50s, Administration).

But if employment can have different effects upon individual self-identities and personal styles, it can also shape expectations of marriage, partner and other personal relationships. In earlier decades it was commonly assumed and, indeed, often expected that (male) managers who were married would subordinate personal and family relationships to their careers (Bell, 1968; Gans, 1967; Whyte, 1960). This was considered to be particularly evident among those who, in the early stages of their careers, were heavily reliant upon the emotional and domestic support of their partners. To a large extent, this pattern persists. Many managers find, for example, that they are forced to disrupt their childrens' education and break up community-based friendships because of the geographical mobility normally associated with career progress (Cohen, 1977; Guerrier and Philpott, 1978). However, as we have already argued, there has been a reassessment of priorities which makes it more likely that managers will now weigh the benefits of promotion against the costs of any personal sacrifices which they may have to make. Consequently, they are more inclined to seek a balance between, on the one hand, the demands of their jobs and their needs for achievement and, on the other, their desire for individual contentment and fulfilling family and personal relationships. There are a number of factors that have brought this about. Perhaps the most important is the more precarious nature of managerial employment and the increased likelihood that their career ambitions will not be achieved. Accordingly, they are more reluctant to commit themselves wholeheartedly to their work particularly if there are high risks of disappointment and if, in addition, it is likely to be detrimental to their wider, personal and family relationships. Although, then, the costs of self-perceived career failure may be high, they can, nevertheless, be contained by developing strategies which limit the extent to which feelings of psychological wellbeing are tied up exclusively with their jobs. More so than in the past, managers may resist the 'greedy' tendencies of their employing organizations and deliberately foster personal identities that are, at least, partially 'independent' of their jobs.

For some men, such personal strategies have been encouraged by the changing attitudes of their partners. In earlier

[137]

decades women were often expected to subordinate and even sacrifice their own employment opportunities. They were generally compelled to neglect their own career interests, to move houses when their husbands accepted promotion and to undertake the domestic responsibilities necessary for 'servicing' their families (Bell, 1968; Pahl and Pahl, 1971). As such, those with jobs relinquished any career opportunities which were available to them and were forced, instead, to seek self-fulfilment either in terms of their domestic roles or, more vicariously, through their husbands' occupational successes (Finch, 1983). Over recent decades, however, the expectations of married middle-class women have changed. Many are now more likely to have their own career ambitions and to insist that the demands of their husbands' jobs are more compatible with these (Rapoport and Rapoport, 1978). As a result, men can less easily assume that their partners will be prepared to organize their lifestyles around their own occupational aspirations. Accordingly, couples attempt to negotiate roles according to which any conflicting priorities can be accommodated.

Of course, the jobs of most managers continue to impose significant constraints upon the development of personal, couple and family relationships. However, it increasingly appears that, there are attempts to resist the potentially all-embracing 'identity-conferring' attributes that corporate responsibilities often impose. Some seem able deliberately to cultivate non-work identities which are explicitly contrary to those required in their jobs. Indeed, there seems to be an emerging trend whereby marriage constitutes a context for the expression of attitudes which are deliberately contrary to those demanded by their employing organizations.[3] For some, then, the relative priorities of work and leisure are reversed. Career interests are subordinated to personal and family priorities and employment is increasingly seen as a means for obtaining the necessary material rewards for obtaining self-fulfilment in private activities and relations outside work. But the extent to which they are able to

[138]

prevent 'spillover' varies. In our study we asked men and women the pre-coded question 'How often do work-related worries preoccupy you during your leisure time and family/ personal life?' Their responses are presented in Figure 6.1.

In the figure, almost half 'sometimes' find that they are preoccupied with work-related issues during their free time. A further 24 per cent of the men and 12 per cent of the women claim this is 'often' the case. Generally speaking, it is the *senior managers* who are more likely to find that preoccupations with work affect their private lives. One in three say that they experience this type of spillover 'often' or

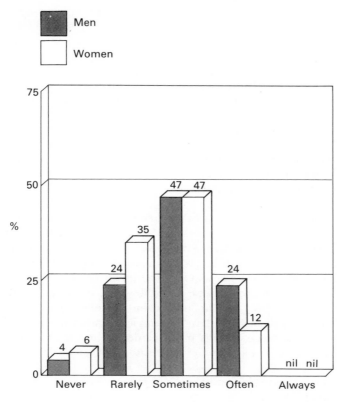

Figure 6.1 Preoccupation with work-related issues during non-working hours.

[139]

'always', compared with only one in five of the middle and junior managers. Even though they may make sustained attempts to separate the two worlds they frequently find that the demands of their jobs become more pervasive as they have been promoted within managerial hierarchies. The following comments reflect this:

> As I've progressed in my career, if you like, it's had an increasing effect. Every time I've moved up a step on the career ladder, it's [work's] intruded just a bit more each time. I would say the situation now is that it probably crowds my home life . . . more than it ever has before . . . You don't walk out of that place and leave it behind. The more responsibility you get, obviously, the more you tend to carry around with you, the more things that are with you going around in your head . . . you get it doing something as mundane as cutting the grass. The task itself doesn't occupy the mind and you usually find that by the time the mower's been up and down the grass a few times, probably what is foremost in your mind, if you're honest, is something at work. It's more likely to be something at work than something at home. So it's in that sort of way that it intrudes, you don't switch it off and forget it . . . I think I recognize the distinction (between home and work) but I'm unable to police it. (male, late 30s, Production).

> I used to, to think of it [work and family] as being fairly black and white until a few years ago. You know, I could never understand those people saying, 'God, I went home last night and couldn't get to sleep, I was thinking about this problem or that problem', you know. Or, 'I was in the bath last night and the solution suddenly came to me about it', as you go up the managerial tree, it [the distinction] becomes greyer . . . You're involved in much more complex decision-making and you come home and it's much harder to, to turn off. You can't stop thinking about it. (male, late 20s, Personnel).

> I must admit I don't take work home, or very rarely, except perhaps in my head . . . perhaps I'm painting or decorating and then I'm tossing things over . . . while I'm watching TV, my mind's often on something else. I get told that sometimes,

'You're not with us – I'm talking to you and you're not listening to me'. And it's true, I'm somewhere else . . . I think most people in my sort of senior category do that, others tend to take work home. (male, late 40s, Production).

I don't think there is a sharp distinction [between home and work] for me. I think I tend to bring quite a lot of work issues into my private time and so, yes, I suppose I do bring work home. I guess I do think a lot about work at home. On the other hand, there probably aren't too many things in my private life that would tend to push things back into the workplace. (male, late 30s, General Management).

At *middle* and *junior* positions, by contrast, there are more managers who are able to maintain sharp boundaries between their work and non-work lives successfully. Only one in three of these managers report that they are 'work' rather than 'home' oriented, by comparison to one in two senior managers. For some, of course both spheres are seen as important in that they offer different, and possibly complementary, ways of achieving personal fulfilment and satisfaction. However, although work is often viewed positively, it is not allowed to intrude upon private lifestyles:

Although I enjoy my work, when I walk out in the evening, it is rare for me to carry about the problems of the office. Immediately I go out of the office door in the evening, I'm thinking about other things, thinking about the home, what I'm going to do in the evening. So I don't live to work by any means . . . I make a very sharp, very sharp indeed, distinction and I find that's probably true of some of my colleagues as well . . . Certainly there is the distinction between what goes on at work and what goes on in the family. It's a very sharp distinction . . . OK, there are going to be occasions when pressures of work are going to create stress that's greater than normal and you're going to worry about something that's going to happen, perhaps the following day. But, once that's out of the way, then there's certainly this cut off. (male, late 30s, Finance and Accounting).

[141]

I would hate to think that I was somebody who lived to work . . . Work is a very important element of my life, meaning that I derive a lot of satisfaction from being successful at it. If I was not successful, I am sure that would spoil that element of my life which is domestically and socially orientated. In other words, success at work is important to me. Then I can switch off and enjoy a normal domestic and social life. (male, late 30s, Sales and Marketing).

I make a very sharp distinction . . . I try not to bring work home . . . I do try to keep work out of my home because to me, you know, home is a very valuable place and the things I like to do here are not necessarily those I like to do at work. So I draw a sharp distinction . . . I'm very lucky, I've always . . . since a young man – been able to switch off, if that's the right terminology. Very rarely do I get preoccupied . . . Yes, I think Sandra would bear me out, that I usually manage to get away from work fairly easily and leave it behind. (male, early 50s, Finance and Accounting).

I'm inclined to live my working life and my home life as totally separate things. Personally, I think its an advantage to be that way. I feel that when you go to work, you haven't had the pressures of work at home and so you work better. And when you come home you can switch off from work and your home life is probably better for it. I like to leave my work at work . . . With a certain amount of work, its not always possible to do. I mean, a certain amount you bring home in your mind. But really, you should leave it at work and not be too concerned about it at home. (male, early 30s, Production).

For other *middle* and *junior* managers – a growing number, we suspect – work is regarded, on balance, as *less* important than non-work personal relationships and home-based lifestyles. It is seen primarily in instrumental terms, as a means for buying resources which enable them to sustain 'alternative' and more self-fulfilling interests. As the following comments illustrate, this kind of orientation is often associated with a reduction in the level of their career aspirations – normally in mid-life – as they become increasingly aware of the highly restricted nature of future opportunities which they have for promotion and of the potentially severe personal costs of remaining ambitious within their jobs. Such feelings are reflected in the following observations:

> I suppose in some ways I've opted out of the rat race. I must admit my work enables me to live and to provide a proper education and upbringing for the children. It's certainly not one hundred per cent work . . . I don't shut home life out at all. I mean . . . you get to a stage in your career when you think you've gone far enough and you've achieved enough – and it's not promotion at all costs. Some people have the drive to go right to the very top and others don't. I'm one of those who don't and I'm quite happy with what I've achieved. It gives us a reasonable standard of living, able to provide the children with more than enough. I'm quite happy. (male, early 40s, Engineering and Maintenance).

> I'm able to detach myself completely when I get home and forget all about it. And it's the family for me. I believe if I go any higher . . . I will be working for the Company 24 hours a day. Then I should be married to the Company. I don't want to marry the Company, I want to stay married to my wife and family. That's it, basically, in a nutshell. Which is why I've got no ambition left. (male, late 40s, Engineering and Maintenance).

> Work is important to me but it's not as important as the home life . . . If I take it down to the basic principles that I've got, it's down to the fact I need to work to provide me with a living wage, so you get down to the basic essentials. I also need work as somewhere to express myself . . . If there's a stress attachment to something that we're doing at work, then, yes, I bring it home . . . if nothing particularly new is going on, then, no, I can quite easily leave that at the desk and it stays there. (male, early 30s, Sales and Marketing).

It seems, then, that senior managers find it more difficult to separate their work and non-work lives than others. This is

[143]

hardly surprising in view of the extent to which their jobs require them to invest high levels of emotional commitment for the purposes of making complex decisions on a day-to-day basis. In this sense, then, they are particularly vulnerable psychologically should they be made redundant. Unlike their junior colleagues they are less able to prevent work influences from pervading almost all other aspects of their lives. Accordingly, if they are made redundant by reason of rationalization, restructuring or corporate takeover they have few or no psychological supports upon which they can fall back.

Seniority, then, is an important consideration in any analysis of the interplay between work and leisure. But what may also be significant in this is the prevailing structures of organizations and the extent to which these affect the work roles of senior managers. In Chapter 3 we discussed how looser organizational forms are gaining greater popularity and, as a result, many corporations are attempting to restructure on these lines. What may be overlooked, however, is the extent to which this can have ramifications not only for the work experiences of managers but also for their private lives. In more loosely structured work settings, as we suggested earlier, there is a need for managers to use a variety of face-to-face, interpersonal skills. Such structures tend to be psychologically more demanding and, as result, managers are more likely to experience stress which will 'spillover' into their private lives. Indeed, it is only when they are at home that they have the time to think clearly about job-related matters. Partners, in turn, are forced into subordinate roles and family and personal lives can be seen as secondary to those of their work interests. Thus, the adoption of less rule-bound forms of organization could have important implications for the home lives of managers which, as yet, have not been fully recognized. Again, this may contribute to their emotional vulnerability should they be made redundant.

Irrespective of seniority and organizational structure, it seems that women are generally less likely than men to have instrumental attitudes towards their work (Marshall, 1984). Yet, as Figure 6.1 suggests, they are also less likely to allow their working experiences to infiltrate their personal lives. To some extent this can be explained by the fact that in our study they are younger than the men and fewer of them are in positions of senior responsibility. Further, roughly one-third are engaged in either personnel or finance/accounting functions. Like most women in management, they are largely removed from core areas of corporate policy and related general management positions where duties and responsibilities are more discretionary and vaguely defined. The high levels of psychological involvement often required in these jobs, coupled with their rather indeterminate nature, tends to foster preoccupations with work problems which can persist during leisure time.

But it is also important to distinguish between those women who are married and those who are single; the former are more inclined to maintain sharp boundaries. Indeed, they are virtually compelled to do so if only because of their domestic responsibilities. But, as we discuss in the next chapter, this is also a function of the psychological contracts which they negotiate with their male partners, most of whom are also in managerial or professional occupations. In fact, if there is any spillover between work and leisure, it is often in the reverse direction; personal and domestic-related anxieties can affect their behaviour at work.[4] Indeed, senior male managers usually put forward such reasons in order to justify their reluctance to promote married women; they express doubts, real or otherwise, about the extent of their 'commitment' and how far they are able to devote themselves wholeheartedly to their jobs and careers (Rothwell, 1985). If women do experience 'spillover' from work into leisure it is more likely to occur among those who are living alone, since they are more inclined to mould their personal identities around their jobs. Work, for them, can be the axis around which they structure their personal relationships. They do not have the domestic commitments of their married women

[145]

colleagues and, as such, their jobs can be more pronounced as central life interests. As two of them comment:

> I do have some sleepless nights, there's no doubt about that . . . occasionally, I throw hysterics at home. A case of thinking, 'Oh God, what am I going to do. How the hell am I going to sort it all out'. . . I'll be sitting and thinking. Subconsciously, it's not conscious, you know, bringing work home. Subconsciously, I'll suddenly get a brainwave . . . and I grab a piece of paper. It does happen. (female, late 20s, Personnel).

> What I often find is if I've got a problem at work and I can't sort it out, normally, I can forget about it for most of the evening. But then, just as I'm getting ready for bed, I'll start thinking about it and normally I can solve it there and then. And I can go back in the next morning and think, 'Yes, I've done it'. . . Yes, I think you do think about work outside. (female, late 20s, Finance).

However, with the exception of a small number of women and of men in senior positions, and those working in less structured work settings, the managers in our study went to great lengths to protect their personal lives from the overriding influences of their jobs. This can be measured in a number of ways: attitudes towards career-related house moves is but one indicator. In the past, married (male) managers seemed readily prepared to accept the personal and family disruption of moving homes if this was linked with, or at least improved, the prospects of promotion (Watson, 1964. Accordingly, they were often willing to subordinate their partners' work interests and the educational needs of their children if their personal rewards were likely to be enhanced. However, it would be surprising if this pattern is as significant today, given the changing nature of family roles and the extent to which men seem less enthusiastic about giving overriding priority to their work and career interests. Thus, it could be expected that fewer of them will be prepared to accept promotion if this is likely to entail a high degree of disturbance in their personal lives (Rozier, 1980). We asked those men participating in our study to assess the significance of various influences which might shape their decisions over career-related moves. In this way, we attempted to identify the relative salience of a variety of factors associated with immediate family and broader community relationships. The results are reported in Figure 6.2.

In terms of the data in Figure 6.2, male managers clearly regard their 'children's education' as a primary consideration when contemplating the implications of career moves. 'Regional differences' in the quality of life and the provision of general amenities are also seen as important. By contrast,

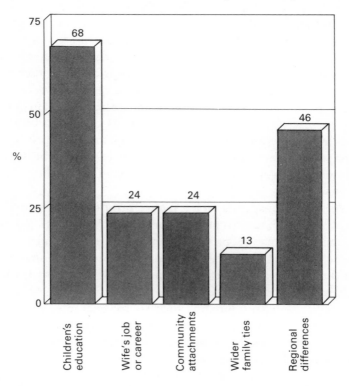

Figure 6.2 Factors affecting career-related house moves (percentage of men assessing factors as 'important' or 'very important').

[147]

'community attachments', 'wider family ties' and 'wife's job or career' are regarded as of less significance in their decision-making. The reasons for the low priority which these men attach to their wives' jobs are not only indicative of the nature of conjugal roles within managerial families but also a reflection of their wives' jobs' generally low material rewards and highly limited career prospects. The priority which they give to their children's education is not surprising given the value attached to credential and meritocratic achievement within middle-class families. But what is, perhaps, interesting is the significance which they attribute to regional factors in planning their future careers. Indeed, this is of growing importance in Britain and reflects the ways in which inequalities in living standards and quality of life are being expressed in regional forms. The north-south divide and the growing impoverishment of some regions means that managers may be reluctant to commit themselves to their careers if they and their families are forced to move into areas where access to high-quality educational, welfare and recreational amenities are perceived to be poor. Even generous relocation benefits can fail to compensate for such anticipated personal costs. The subsequent immobility of managers is likely to become a growing problem if regional inequalities in the quality of life persist.[5]

As male managers attach a higher priority to their private lives and attempt to protect these from work-related influences, the nature of their *homes* change. Of course, for those who are unable to resist these pressures, the home may be little more than a refuge within which managers simply unwind, relax and indulge in various passive or non-participative leisure pursuits such as, for example, watching television. In this context, the significant recent growth in the *domestic* consumption of alcohol may be an expression of the physical and psychological costs which they pay in order to cope with the transition between work and home in ways which reduce personal tension and facilitate 'relaxation' (Hunt and Collins, 1983). But for those who are able to achieve a separation between home and work successfully, and who regard their jobs in primarily instrumental terms, their domestic settings may be becoming more important as locales where self-fulfilment can be obtained through the exercise of talents and skills which are underutilized in their jobs. In these circumstances, the home is a sphere of *resistance* rather than simply a refuge or retreat.[6] It comes to represent a private arena which must be protected against encroachments from the world of work; a place where individuals, alone or with others, may pursue a variety of interests and pursuits which they find psychologically more engaging than their jobs. To gain some insight into these contrasting uses of leisure time we asked the managers in our study to indicate the frequency of their involvement in different pastimes during a typical seven-day period, on a five-point scale ranging from 'never' to 'always'. Their answers are reported in Figure 6.3.

For managers, like most people, 'passive relaxation' – in particular, watching television – remains a popular, or at least a time-consuming activity. By contrast, few seem to be regularly engaged in community affairs or to socialize with business colleagues or clients; only about 10 per cent state 'often' or 'always' for these activities. In many ways, this pattern is compatible with their desire to maintain private and home-centred lifestyles. They choose *not* to become involved in local activities on the grounds that they spend most of their working lives 'handling people', 'solving problems' and 'trying to get others to do things'. Given the demands and stresses of these managerial tasks it is scarcely surprising that the organizational demands of voluntary and community associations are of limited appeal. Similarly, those who wish to separate their private and working lives are unlikely to want to spend much of their spare time entertaining business colleagues or clients. Instead, most of them prefer to be alone or to devote any available time to their immediate families. Consequently, almost 30 per cent claim they engage in 'active hobbies with other family members' 'often' or 'always'

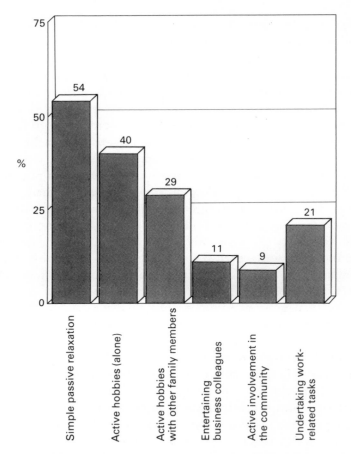

Figure 6.3 Managers' leisure pursuits (percentage reporting different activities as 'often' or 'always').

during the course of a typical week and over 40 per cent also say that they follow such pursuits with similar regularity, but *alone*.

The relative popularity of these activities would seem to confirm the view that many managers meet their needs for self-fulfilment *outside* work. If a sense of achievement or personal development is denied them in their jobs, it can at least be acquired through such diverse activities as gardening,

[150]

house repair, sculpture, painting, sport, car restoration, model building, cooking, script writing, preparing computer software, walking, hill climbing, touring, visiting art galleries and museums. Indeed, these are just some of the more active leisure pursuits which managers described to us in our interviews. Despite their varied nature, most of these pursuits require the exercise of creativity and a considerable level of psychological involvement. Indeed, if the enthusiasm with which they describe these activities is any measure, then, in our view, many managers would seem to be reserving their energies for leisure rather than for work. More generally, the changing pattern of non-work interests lends some support to this. If during the immediate postwar decades free time was primarily geared to passively 'being entertained', now it is more likely to involve active participation. The boom in middle-class 'health sports' such as jogging, aerobics, weight training, tennis and squash; in such home-based 'hi-tech' activities as computer games and film-making; and in 'activity holidays' such as golf, horseriding, walking, wind-surfing and skiing, all bear witness to a growing preference for challenging and self-fulfilling free-time pursuits (Leisure Consultants, 1986). Certainly, these contrast sharply with the leisure patterns of those who, preoccupied with their jobs and unable to carve out 'private' spheres of autonomy, do little but watch television, daydream, or habitually consume alcohol.

But what of managers' partners? How do they respond to the preferences and preoccupations of their spouses? We consider these in some detail in the next chapter. Here, in order to conclude this discussion, we briefly explore how far male managers 'incorporate' their partners in their careers and share with them their work-related problems (Finch, 1983). Those who took part in our study were asked to assess, on a five-point scale, ranging from 'not at all relevant' to 'very relevant', a number of statements describing their relationships with their wives. The results are reported in Figure 6.4.

[151]

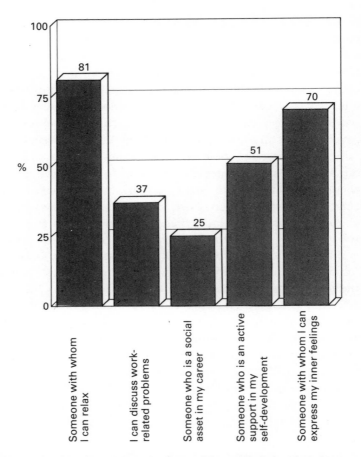

Figure 6.4 Male managers' relationships with their wives (percentage describing these as 'relevant' or 'very relevant').

Just over one-third regard their relationship with their partners as important for discussing work-related problems (they score either 4 or 5). However, more than 80 per cent refer, in a similar manner, to their wives as 'someone with whom they can express their inner feelings'. Although these responses only offer a crude indication, they do suggest that most men managers do not expect their wives to be interested in, or to make any significant contribution to, their careers. Such findings, then, lead us to question the extent to which they are psychologically immersed in their husbands' jobs. Managers' wives are, perhaps, no longer required to share their husbands' work-related problems extensively or to be socially involved in different aspects of corporate life (Pahl and Pahl, 1971). Instead, they are encouraged by their husbands to maintain 'a safe distance' from the demands of their jobs. Above all, they are seen as custodians of the private sphere and protectors of lifestyles and home-based indentities which are separate from and, indeed, resistant to the potentially all-pervasive influences of managerial work.

Male managers, then, particularly those in middle and junior positions, are attempting to redefine the character of their private lives. If, in the past, these were often regarded as secondary to their organizational careers, this is now less likely to be the case. As organizations are restructured, career paths restricted, and job security undermined, managers are becoming more cautious about committing themselves fully to their jobs. Accordingly, it is not altogether surprising that they are developing more instrumental orientations towards their employing organizations and searching, to a greater extent than in the past, for self-fulfilment *outside* work. They look, as we have shown, to leisure pursuits, home life, and personal relationships. Thus, the influence of their partners is becoming more significant. We turn our attention to them in the next chapter.

Notes

1 Marxist writers normally start from this assumption arguing that capitalist relations of production and distribution inevitably create alienated labour.
2 Hence, attempts to improve the 'quality of working life' through redesigning jobs by establishing more broadly defined work tasks.

3 In our in-depth interviews it was noticeable that our respondents went to great lengths to 'present themselves' – in language, style and appearance – in ways that were in sharp contrast to their *personae* at work.
4 These can be associated as much with the caring needs of elderly parents as with those of children; a dimension of lifestyle which is often overlooked in discussions of women managers.
5 With, of course, important ramifications for the quality of management in organizations located within more depressed geographical areas.
6 'Resistance' in the sense of acting out lifestyles and adhering to attitudes and beliefs which are strikingly incongruent with those expected of them within corporate settings.

CHAPTER 7

Men and women managers and their partners

In general, the nature of managers' conjugal and personal relationships have been neglected in studies of their lifestyles. This was particularly the case in earlier decades when, even more than today, the overwhelming majority of corporate managers were men. If there were any discussions of managers' personal relationships these tended to focus on the ways in which their partners performed a variety of domestic tasks which aided and supported them in their careers (Bell, 1968; Pahl and Pahl, 1971; Whyte, 1960). The structure and composition of managerial families, therefore, were seen to be compatible with the needs for geographical mobility normally associated with career advance. Thus, in the 1960s, it was argued that the 'isolated', two-generational nuclear family was functional for managerial success (Parsons, 1964). However, some writers did query such claims on the basis of research findings which suggested that broader kin linkages were of continuing importance in the middle class and that the 'isolated' or 'privatized' nature of their family patterns had been greatly exaggerated (Litwak, 1961). Indeed, there was the accumulation of evidence which demonstrated the significance of 'neighbourhood' networks for structuring personal relationships among male managers, their wives and children (Gans, 1967). 'Suburbia as a way of life' was seen to depict the emergence of new 'classless' patterns of behaviour within the rapidly growing prosperous residential areas of the

[155]

1950s and 1960s. How, then, were managers' wives supposed to fit into this 'new' reality?

As a result of the emotional, psychological and material support which they were expected to offer in their roles as homemakers, managers' wives were generally expected to relinquish any claims on jobs and careers. It was often assumed that if they did have any work ambitions, these should be deferred until their children had left home or school. In practice, of course, this meant that most found they could only obtain jobs with limited prospects because they had missed various promotion opportunities and were regarded by employers as 'too old' to embark upon careers. It was, then, hardly suprising that successful career women tended to be single rather than married (Marshall, 1984). Whereas the delineation of roles within managerial families reinforced the work and career orientations of husbands, it offered little for the employment prospects of wives. Thus, excluded as they were from the more highly paid and prestigious jobs, managers' wives were forced to develop personal identities based upon patterns of consumption (Finch, 1983). They were normally regarded as the principal purchasers of consumer goods, produced to meet the needs of this expanding socio-economic group. Thus, they became the main marketing target of advertisers, since it was they who made the major decisions about the purchase of most household items. It was, then, to be expected that when television advertising was introduced in Britain, broadcasting companies organized their programming schedules around the interests of women.[1] At the same time, managers' wives were often regarded as 'symbols' of consumption, expressing their husbands' career success through their personal appearance and lifestyles. Accordingly, they could be perceived as pursuing careers of *consumption* in ways which were compatible with their husbands' achievements within the occupational order. Indeed, a failure to achieve or sustain such congruence could result in the breakdown of their marriages.

It is for these reasons, it was argued, that managers' wives were 'incorporated' within their husbands' jobs and that they, too, pursued careers albeit in a derived and 'vicarious' manner (Finch, 1983). Thus, they were expected not only to support their husbands within the context of family relations but also to contribute more explicitly to their spouses' careers through entertaining business colleagues and by acting as their 'ambassadors' at various social and work-related gatherings. Indeed, senior managers in many large companies encouraged such practices by interviewing wives when appointing men to managerial positions. As a result of their derived identities, many managers' wives, experienced feelings of success or failure according primarily to their husbands' achievements.

It was not until the late 1960s that such views began to be challenged.[2] Increasing numbers of better qualified, younger women started to react against expectations that they should relinquish their own career prospects in favour of their husbands' jobs (Oakley, 1982). Their views fuelled campaigns for 'rights' in relation to abortion, childcare and workplace equality: all issues which were of particular concern to women who were young, middle-class and embarking upon organizational careers. Thus, the women's movement particularly appealed to those who wished to challenge prevailing views about middle-class lifestyles and the roles that women were expected to fulfil. As a result, younger women today see their futures differently compared with two decades ago. More of them now expect good career prospects, choosing not to get married and to avoid (or defer) having children if this will hinder their job opportunities (Cooper and Davidson, 1982; Marshall, 1984). Among those who do marry, there are changing expectations and assumptions about the division of family responsibilities, child rearing, and husband–wife relationships (Rapoport and Rapoport, 1976). They are now more likely to be assertive in their personal ambitions and to pursue work and leisure interests which are less heavily dependent upon their husbands' preferences. Even though in material terms the lifestyles of most managers' wives remain overwhelmingly shaped by their husbands' jobs, their psychological 'incorporation' can be much reduced. In the late 1970s, for example, Handy (1978) found that managers' wives displayed little interest in their husbands' jobs. Even among male executives in 'conventional' marriages.

> The wife tends to be generally supportive of her husband in his work, although she does not show too much interest or involvement in its details. It is not a shared area. One wife . . . a very supportive one, did not, in fact, know what her husband's job was, although she did know the name of his employers. (p.40).

In our interviews, we found that only one in three of the managers' wives ever discuss work-related matters with their husbands and that only a small minority undertake any kind of home entertaining for their partners' colleagues.[3] As we discussed in the previous chapter, many try to sustain domestic roles which resist the psychological demands of their husbands' jobs and, as such, they attempt to remain emotionally detached from their day-to-day work-related preoccupations. Indeed, few wives appear to know *precisely* what their husbands do at work, in terms of the nature of their jobs, duties and responsibilities, and have little idea of their particular career ambitions. They prefer, instead, to maintain sharp divisions between home and work spheres so that personal relationships are protected from the potentially greedy demands of employing organizations. The following comments illustrate such strategies:

> I suppose it [his career] has made me think about what I should do with myself occasionally. Because there have been times in the past when he has been extremely busy. So, therefore, I've had to develop a certain life of my own, I suppose. Perhaps it's made me a little more independent than I may otherwise have been . . . I've never felt part of it – I've never felt I was supporting him but I've never felt obliged to entertain on his behalf or that sort of thing. That's never

arisen . . . But, no, not actually involved in his world as such – I don't understand it as much as anything else. It is a very specialized field and unless you actually work in it, it's very difficult to understand . . . I suppose, too, when you're really involved in management, the wife takes over the home responsibilities from you which you might otherwise feel involved in. (partner of male, late 40s, Computing).

I wouldn't be content at all to sit at home and wait for the pearls from his lips or whatever because he doesn't involve me in his work that much anyway . . . I know very little about what he does from the time he goes in the morning to when he comes home. (partner of male, early 40s, Production).

We never discuss his work, no. It's a bit too complicated for me. It's not the kind of work you can sit down and discuss anyway. Some of it is very confidential. (partner of male, late 30s, General Management).

No, Jim doesn't bring his problems home. If there's a house move to be made that affects us all, then, it's discussed but, no, he doesn't bring his work home. We sometimes talk about major issues, but day-to-day problems, no. (partner of male, late 30s, Administration).

I would prefer him to be at work to do his work and then come home and relax than come home and work from home . . . I enjoy it when he's home, but I think I would prefer him to do all his work at work and then come home and relax and try and switch off from work. (partner of male, early 30s, Administration).

These women, then, do not see themselves as exclusively involved with their husbands' work preoccupations. They accept they are living with men who have demanding jobs but who undertake these in organizational settings about which they, as wives, know little. Indeed, the implementation of various forms of 'new' technology could be reinforcing this trend since it often enhances the more specialist and technical nature of managerial jobs and thereby reduces the

[159]

extent to which husbands and wives are able to discuss work-related issues.[4] Many women, then, feel only marginally involved in their husbands' work; their jobs are perceived as part of a world which is external to the marriage relationship and in which they have no role. Of course, despite explicit attempts to resist work-related pressures some wives do become reluctantly involved in their husbands' career-related problems and consequently find that these intrude into their personal lives (Evans and Bartolomé, 1980). Within our study a particularly striking and exceptional pattern was evident amongst the wives of those managers employed by the banking and financial services organization. As part of its corporate strategy this company, in common with many other financial institutions, deliberately fosters a high level of community involvement. As such, the roles of bank managers, for example, are more broadly defined and incorporate a variety of non-work as well as work expectations (Finch, 1983). Irrespective of their personal preferences, therefore, wives often become involved in their husbands' occupationally related activities. If, in earlier decades, this may have offered a source of personal pride it now can serve as a source of irritation and personal anxiety; confirming, perhaps, that such expectations are contrary to present-day prevailing assumptions. The following comments, from one of the wives, illustrate these concerns:

> We never mention banking when we're on holiday. If it has come out, well, people treat you different then. It annoys me, it's a sore point with me . . . The number of people I've had to say, 'Look, I'm Maureen Jones, I'm not a bank manager's wife.' I don't like it, I'm a character in my own right . . . But I wouldn't be in any other position. I've enjoyed living in this town. We've got to know quite a lot of people down here, purely because of being in banking . . . Belonging to organizations, you get invites, and people invite you because you're the bank manager's wife. It's nice, that side of it, I enjoy it . . . Our longest friends are banking people, funnily enough. (partner of male, late 30s, General Management).

[160]

Clearly, there are contradictions in these comments. On the one hand, there is resentment of a vicarious identity and yet, on the other, recognition that it facilitates social contacts and access to various organizational and community activities. Thus, despite any attempts to the contrary, some women may be psychologically and socially trapped by their husbands' jobs and any attempts to develop more independent personal identities are severely curtailed.[5] As the wives of two managers remark:

> If you're in a small community, the bank manager is one of the people that people turn to, like the schoolmaster and the vicar, you know. And, as part of that set-up, you are the bank manager's wife and you're looked upon in that sort of way . . . Everyone knows who you are and you have to shop in certain places and all that business, a certain church, even. (partner of male, early 50s, General Management).

> It's interesting because a lot of wives identify very much with the bank. A lot of their mutual friends are banking friends and it seems that it is even so with wives and children as well, perhaps. (partner of male, early 30s, Administration).

However, the experiences of these women are exceptional; most of those in our survey are able to cultivate personal relationships, lifestyles and self-identities which are partially removed, at least, from the pressures of their husbands' jobs. This seems to be particularly the case for many of those whose husbands work in public sector organizations. These appear to be less 'greedy' in their demands on the personal lives of managers who are less inclined to take work home or share job-related problems with their wives. This can be a reason why those who are professionally or technically qualified, such as accountants and computer technologists, choose to work in public rather than private sector organizations.[6] Indeed, they are often prepared to forgo higher salaries and fringe benefits for the advantages of less occupationally related lifestyles. However, this is *not* to imply

[161]

that they are subject to fewer pressures than their private sector colleagues. On the contrary, our impression is that, as a result of government fiscal policies, the introduction of strict methods of budgetary control and reductions in staff levels, they often work harder and are subject to greater pressures. One senior manager in the public sector draws the following comparison:

> Having had experience of working in the private sector and the public sector, there is definitely a different attitude. The firm I worked for was a leading firm of chartered accountants. It was very good, an extremely good company . . . In all honesty, it was my best employer, you know, in terms of financial remuneration and care for you. If you were on the way up, you know, they looked after you extremely well because it was in their interest to do so. But, in return, they expect loyalty and definitely, it was the job first and the family afterwards. At the same time, there's another aspect to it – your social life also came into the fore. You were expected to entertain clients and, if necessary, put them up overnight or take them out to the theatre. You often invited the client back home . . . I'll put my hand on my heart, I'll be quite open about it, it's an easier life in the public sector than in the private sector, there's less pressure and less demands on your private life; of pursuing the client, the firm's role, you know of acting as an ambassador for the firm. It's far less in this job. (male, early 40s, Finance and Accounting).

Even in the private sector fewer companies now expect managers and their partners to entertain business colleagues. To an extent, this is in response to the changing expectations which women have of their marital roles and of their own personal identities. In addition, of course, far more married women now have their own jobs. The growth of clerical and service occupations, the increasing acquisition of academic qualifications and professional skills, and the changing aspirations of many women have dramatically increased the numbers working in part-time and full-time jobs (Goffee and Scase, 1985). In our own study, 59 per cent of all managers' wives have jobs but, of these, 60 per cent work part-time; of all wives, only 24 per cent (176) have full-time jobs. The distribution of these is shown in Figure 7.1.

In line with the common pattern, these women are over-whelmingly employed in either lower-grade professional and administrative jobs or in various routine clerical, sales and non-manual occupations. Examples of the former include social work, school teaching, office administration and other similar jobs, primarily located within the state sector; the

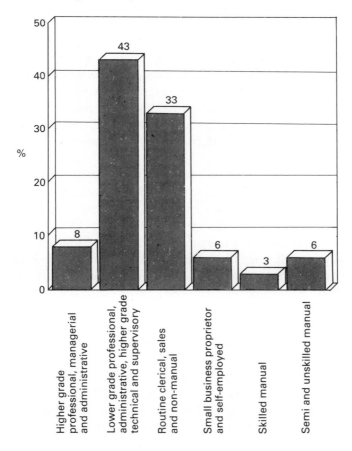

Figure 7.1 The occupations of male managers' partners.

[163]

latter include secretaries, shop assistants, sales representatives, receptionists and so on. Clearly, few of these offer, or are perceived to provide, career opportunities. This is in sharp contrast to the husbands of the women managers we interviewed, who, to a far greater extent, are employed in various managerial and professional occupations which have traditionally offered relatively good career prospects. Thus, whereas women managers are likely – *if* they are married – to be in so-called dual-career families, this is not normally the case for male managers (Rapoport and Sierakowski, 1982). But, if the wives of male managers are predominantly in non-career jobs, what are their motives for employment? Are they simply working because of financial pressures or are they seeking additional psychological rewards (Dunnell, 1979; Eurostat, 1981)? In order to explore this issue we asked a precoded question which attempted to assess the extent to which various financial, career and other related factors influenced employment decisions. The responses are reported in Figure 7.2.

Financial considerations are clearly a major reason why some managers' wives have jobs, while less than 10 per cent are reported to appear explicitly concerned to develop careers. Indeed, from our interviews it is apparent that many wives work to help pay school fees, to save for holidays and to pay for different 'non-essential' items. Nevertheless, most of them work primarily for non-financial reasons associated with the need to develop interests, relationships and lifestyles that offer, if only to a limited degree, personal independence and self-fulfilment. Indeed, even part-time, poorly-paid occupations which offer little scope for intrinsic interest can enable them partially to escape the identity conferring attributes of their husbands' occupations.[7]

Even so, male managers appear to attach only limited importance to the occupational needs and aspirations of their wives. When assessing the relative significance of various non-work factors on deciding whether or not to make career-related house moves, for example, more than two-

[164]

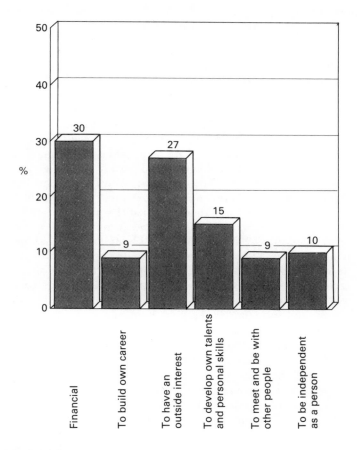

Figure 7.2 Why managers' wives work.

thirds of those in our survey take account of the possible repercussions for their children's education whereas less than a quarter regard any impact upon their wives' jobs as important. In a sense, their responses are shaped, at least to some extent, by the limited career prospects and relatively low pay of their wives' jobs, but even those women who attempt to retain their career ambitions frequently find that

[165]

these are frustrated by their husbands' priorities. The following exchange illustrates the problems:

Wife: His job has wrecked it [my career] completely. When we got married, we settled in York, that was my home town, and I got a job in the civil service. I had to because he'd opted to go into local government for the security but the money he got, what was it, £600. So I had to work and I went in as a clerical officer in the Department of Employment. I was recommended for promotion as early as I could be, the soonest panel I could go on. I got on it and I got through. The manager there said I would go far and the only far I've gone is travelling round with Trevor. I got promotion again but before I got an appointment he'd moved to Cornwall. There are poor prospects down there, so I had to wait two years for promotion. I had it for about a year and he moved to Kent. So I managed to get a transfer to Kent. I hung on there and just when they said I was ready for the panel for a higher grade, he moved to Sussex. So, instead of going up, I went down a grade because there were no vacancies and so I had to go back to the promotion board again. Barely had I had promotion for a year and we'd moved back to Kent again . . . There's a possibility of a vacancy but I'm sort of waiting at home . . . but it's only clerical again.

Husband:. . . I've always put my own career first.

Wife: Yes, there can't be two careers in a family.

Husband: But we always talk it over.

Wife: It's always a mutual decision.

Husband: I'd never put in for a job off my own bat. We always talk it out and decide whether or not I should go for it . . . I feel guilty that her career has suffered because I know she is very clever and it's unfair on her. I mean, going for the job that she is going for now, a clerical job. Good God, that's not really for her, but it's the price we pay, unfortunately.

Wife: . . . My ambition now is to get back to work and start afresh. They showed me the job, I can't say it looks interesting because it isn't. But I can't stay at home all day . . . I haven't got any hobbies . . . I've been roped in for flower arranging at the church up the road and that sort of thing, but I'm afraid it isn't enough . . . I have an active brain, I would say. I also like to be with people and do something on my own. (male, late 30s, Administration; and partner).

[166]

As this account illustrates, when men are *forced* to be geographically mobile because of career-related moves, it usually disrupts their wives' occupational opportunities and compels them to search for jobs which are lower paid and which offer few or no prospects. At the same time, senior managers are reluctant to recruit or promote married women into positions of responsibility because of their assumption that they will be unable to commit themselves to jobs for a substantial period (Alban-Metcalfe and Nicholson, 1984). Accordingly, even the most ambitious women may find that they are restricted to boring and low-paid jobs. This can lead to anger and bitterness and make husbands feel guilty. Even so, both partners often share the view that mens' careers take priority and that womans' thwarted ambitions are the necessary price that has to be paid. It is in these terms that the opinions of their husbands must be interpreted. While many of them seem keen for their partners to have jobs, few are prepared to allow their wives' career ambitions to interfere with what they already consider to be their own very limited prospects (Finch, 1983). When asked to rank on a five-point scale their feelings of how far their wives' employment has affected the quality of their marital and family lives, less than one-tenth claim the consequences have been either 'negative' or 'very negative', while over two-thirds argue the effects have been 'positive' or 'very positive'. In view of our earlier comments, it is perhaps not surprising that managers in the banking and financial services organization are exceptional in their lack of enthusiasm for their wives having jobs and for feeling that these adversely affect the quality of family relationships.

So far, we have discussed how wives are able to cultivate relatively autonomous home lives which are resistant to the demands of their partners' work organizations. But what of the male partners of *women* managers? It is hardly likely that they will be prepared to relinquish career ambitions, redefine their own jobs as of 'secondary importance' and give priority to domesticity in their lifestyles. Indeed, this may explain

[167]

why far fewer women managers *have* partners (Davidson and Cooper, 1983). Among those in our study, for example, only 55 per cent are married or living with a partner compared with more than 95 per cent of the men. The occupational distribution of these husbands or partners is shown in Figure 7.3.

Almost 80 per cent are employed in various types of managerial, professional and technical jobs; occupations, that

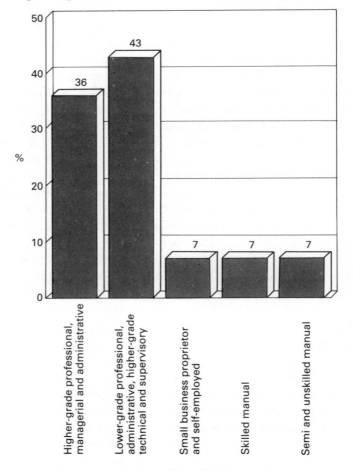

Figure 7.3 The occupations of female managers' partners.

[168]

is, which offer relatively good salaries and which have *traditionally* been perceived to have career prospects. Unlike male managers, then, the careers of these women managers are more likely to be interrupted because of the demands of their partners' jobs. Four in ten claim their own career prospects have been jeopardized for this reason and, of these, one in two feels 'very resentful'. Further, while only one in ten of the married male managers in our study consider their wives' jobs to be 'very important' in deciding whether or not they should move homes to further their career prospects, no less than one in two of the women managers regard this factor as 'very important'. It would seem, then, that among couples where both partners are in managerial or professional jobs there is a tendency for mens' interests to take priority over those of women (Gowler and Legge, 1982). The self-fulfilling prophecy which limits women's occupational success is complete when senior male managers in large-scale corporations are reluctant to promote married women because they perceive them to be less geographically mobile and, therefore, by comparison with men, less suitable for appointment to responsible positions.

However, there is a prevailing view among married women managers that their own career commitments generally contribute to, rather than detract from, harmonious personal relationships with their partners; over 70 per cent claim that the effects are either 'positive' or 'very positive'. How, then, do women cope with the potential conflicts between career demands and their private and family lives? A number of strategies are available, ranging from negotiating appropriate conjugal roles and 'planning' for children, to hiring domestic assistance. Women are often better able to make these arrangements if they launch their careers *before* living with someone on a permanent basis. Conjugal roles then become structured in ways which allow each of the partners to respond flexibly to particular job demands. In these circumstances, it is only in the last instance – when, for example, the acceptance of promotion demands job mobility

– that the careers of male partners take precedence. By contrast, partners who are not in career-related occupations tend to become locked into domestic relationships and progressively develop, during the duration of their marriages, non-work self-identities. If, at any stage, they attempt to embark upon their own careers, this can often place considerable stress on their marriages, leading in extreme cases to break-up and divorce. In sum, for women who embark upon careers before choosing a partner, conjugal roles become imposed upon dual-career assumptions. For others, later career ambitions must develop within the context of conjugal expectations which tend to inhibit or restrain any such aspirations. The extent to which women can successfully sustain harmonious domestic relationships in ways which are compatible with the needs of their careers is reflected in the following observations:

> I met my husband when I was 20, we met and married in 6 months . . . But when I met him, obviously we talked, started talking about things and I said, 'Look, don't think I'm stopping, you know, getting married to you and finishing work, end of story.' And we are a fortunate couple in that we can talk to each other and I said, 'Well, look, I don't feel that I want children at the moment, I may change my mind in the future, but, at the moment, my career means everything to me.' He accepted that and said, 'Right, fair enough . . .' If you ask him now, he's more strongly against having children than I am because he's got used to our way of life without children and he knows it could not be the same with children. We enjoy foreign holidays, a car and doing what we want when we want to, not the same drudge of cooking for the children or whatever. If I come home from work and we've had a hard day, well, we go out for a meal, whereas with children, that would not be the case . . . Certainly, my personal life is very important to me . . . Certainly I feel I've got this balance whereby nothing gets in the way. I'm not losing anything from my personal life. Because I'm happy in my work and I'm satisfied in my job, it enhances my personal life in that I'm a happier person in myself . . . My husband's been fantastic . . . I think it depends upon the man, it depends

upon the husband. If my husband was such that he expected his tea on the table at six o'clock, it wouldn't work, our marriage wouldn't work . . . I really think I wouldn't benefit by being a single person. I've benefited by having a husband in the sense that when I do want to talk about something, he's here, even if it's going in one ear and out of the other, you're talking to somebody as opposed to talking to the wall which could send you bananas . . . You know, you're there for each other in that respect to support each other, I think. Certainly, I don't suffer from having a husband, I really think it's more of a benefit to me than anything else. (female, late 20s, Finance and Accounting).

Our careers are equally important. They always have been. There've been times when he has been more successful than I've been successful and vice versa . . . I suppose it will end up fairly equal one day. So both careers are important . . . I think we've been very lucky. The biggest compromise we've ever made is when I left the Post Office for a new job. My job was in Banbury and his was in the City and we lived in Oxford. That was quite a compromise because he had to commute by train into the City every day . . . But it wasn't a compromise, it was a happy consensus . . . No, we haven't had to compromise at all.
Interviewer: Do you see a time in the future when the two careers would come into serious conflict?
I don't think so because of the basis of our relationship . . . It might be foolhardy to say, 'Of course not', but I think it's dependent upon the nature of the relationship you have. I think we both know where each other wants to go. I think if he was answering the questions, he would say that he would expect me to be more successful than him. I'm not actually sure he's right. People plateau at different times, you know, but that's what he expects or could anticipate. We're quite happy if that would happen and vice versa. (female, late 20s, Personnel).

For these women, at least, there appear to be few irrecon-cilable conflicts between marital and work roles. They have chosen to live with men who recognize the importance of their careers and with whom they have established satisfactory forms of mutual adjustment. However, although couples may be capable of maintaining compatible lifestyles, difficulties can arise when there are children. Among the fifty-one women managers in our survey, only ten have children; three of them each have one, six have two, and one has three. *All* of the married women recognize that having children can seriously jeopardize careers, often to the extent that it might require them to resign their jobs. Even with hired domestic assistance most feel that the demands of child rearing on the one hand, and those of career pursuit on the other, are generally incompatible. The personal dilemmas which this creates for women are well captured in the following reflections:

> I think it's very, very difficult . . . You need a lot of help. I mean, you need not just the support and help from your husband and understanding from your family, but I think you also need physical help in running the house . . . You've got to have a very understanding and supportive husband. But it's quite difficult. I think that somebody who tries it without a lot of back-up, either a full-time nanny or a cleaner, to bring up a family is extremely difficult because you're just rushing from one sort of scheduling to another . . . There's never a time to relax. I think it's very difficult to combine a career and you've got to be very single-minded if you want to do it. (female, early 50s, General Management).

> Well, I think it's difficult [having children] . . . I'm a bit torn about it. I'm very aware that I'm getting older and whilst I don't feel a great need for children now and I'm not at all maternal, I've always been one where the grass is always greener and I know that once I reach the magic age of 35, when I'm too old, I may suddenly want them and my career will diminish in importance at that stage. Maybe, maybe in a year or two, but I've been saying that for years. I prefer not to think about it, and think about it tomorrow, which I know is a negative approach but I don't have the answer. I sometimes think I would quite like to have a child and support it myself outside a marriage. It would present a load of problems, I know, but maybe that would suit me better as an indi-

vidual . . . If you're committed to a career you've got, somewhere along the line, you've got to decide what comes first, the family or the career and you cannot just split them 50–50. To most working women who have a family, the family has to come first . . . I think you have a lot of problems as a mother and a careerist to be honest with you. Not least of all from your kid. (female, early 30s, Administration).

I fully believe that I will have children one day but it won't be until I'm very old. You know, very old for children. I certainly believe I will do that one day. I cannot see me working until I'm say, 55 . . . I've always said that once I've finished work to have children, I don't want to go back to work unless necessary because of finances . . . I would want to see the children grow up . . . I don't believe children benefit with working mothers. I've always said that once I do have children, then that's it. That is why we have said we will do everything now before we have children and before I give up work . . . The disadvantage as well is if you do go back to work after, say, five years, things change so much. I might go back in at the same level but you're going to feel a bit of a dumbo in the sense that everything will have changed . . . So, I really think you would suffer by going back. It would take a hell of a lot to pick up the threads again. (female, late 20s, Finance and Accounting).

I don't think both parents can be in full-time work, out of the house, and bring up children. I think perhaps, I'm old-fashioned, but I think children ought to be brought up by a parent, with a parent around. On the other hand, I don't always see why it should be the woman. As far as I'm concerned, I couldn't bear to be stuck indoors looking after a brat; that would drive me round the twist being cooped up all the time. But why should it be a sacrifice for the one who decides to stay home if that's what he or she wants to do? But I suppose I'm out of line in fashionable thinking in that way. (female, early 30s, Engineering and Maintenance).

As these accounts suggest, the tensions associated with having children cannot be overcome simply by hiring domestic help since this does not resolve the problem of having *time* to establish and sustain emotional and affective ties. Even *with* time, some women express anxiety about the potential conflict which can result from the perceived need to be 'tough' and 'assertive' in their role as managers and 'caring' and 'affectionate' in their role as mothers.[8]

In general, our evidence indicates that most women managers cope with any potential conflicts between their work and home lives by not having children and by choosing to live with partners who are prepared to accommodate the demands of their two careers. In addition, it often appears that dual-career couples agree to protect their non-work lives from the threat of work-related preoccupations by drawing clear boundaries between home and work and maintaining sharp distinctions between their professional and personal identities. Married women managers, then, may be strongly committed to their jobs but not to the extent that they allow these to dominate their personal lives. On the contrary, in common with many married men, they explicitly nurture domestic lifestyles which are resistant to work-related pressures. When asked to assess, on a five-point scale, the relevance of various statements describing the nature of their relationships with their partners no fewer than 75 per cent emphasize their importance as 'someone with whom I can express inner feelings'. By contrast, fewer than 40 per cent see them as 'someone with whom I can discuss work-related problems'. Our interviews confirm the extent to which they maintain a sharp distinction between their work and domestic lives and, thereby, resist the potential for occupational 'spillover'.

> Once I walk through the door, that's it. I've switched off. I just can't think about work at home and I don't want to change that . . . It's always been that way. It's incredible, I really wouldn't want to lose that gift . . . I don't see work as taking any more or less weight than it has or taking up any more time than it has. I was never a workaholic to start with. In fact, if having a successful career meant becoming a workaholic, then, no thank you very much. I suppose it's fair

to say that I'm only as successful as I have been because it has come with the effort I'm prepared to make. It's not the be-all and end-all of my life in any way. (female, early 30s, Engineering and Maintenance).

I drink and smoke quite a lot and I know from reading the evidence that people like me at work, female managers at my sort of level, are the fastest growing smoking population in the country. I think it's true. Probably drink could well be a problem for a lot of my colleagues and me. But I also switch off completely and we're [my husband and I] very indulgent. I'm not houseproud and we play tennis and we watch cricket and we do what we want at weekends . . . And my husband, I mean he really is the best example of what feminism is trying to achieve because he has a total equality approach to life, far more than most men I know and so there aren't the stresses here. (female, late 20s, Personnel).

Unless I have to do some work, I don't think about office work at home. I've a lot of other things which occupy my time . . . and I never talk about work with Paul although he was in the same organization for a long time, you know. We never discuss work at all . . . . Work stays outside the home except for the occasions when I, fairly rare now, when I do work at home. (female, early 50s, General Management).

It seems, then, that many married women managers, like their male colleagues, regard their partners as individuals with whom they can create and sustain *distinctive* non-work roles and identities. Very few couples are totally immersed in their work and overwhelmingly preoccupied with career success. Certainly, many are committed to their jobs and would like to be successful in their careers, but not to the extent of undermining their personal and family relationships. Accordingly, conflicts between work and domestic life are controlled; at least on a day-to-day basis. They tend to emerge only when the offer of promotion requires men to be geographically mobile or when choices have to be made about having children.

[175]

In the light of these findings, how much has changed for marriage partners since the 1950s and 1960s? Generalizations are difficult if only because of variations which are linked to stages in family and life cycles (Dunnell, 1979; Young and Willmott, 1973). The attitudes, values and behavioural patterns of newly married childless couples in their mid-20s, for example, are likely to be very different from those of couples in their mid-40s with teenage children. Similarly, differences in occupational roles and career orientations significantly shape the negotiation of marriage relationships among conjugal partners. Nevertheless, it is possible to detect two emerging models of conjugal roles. The first is the dual-career couple where, typically, both partners have embarked on careers before living together; have carefully selected each other in terms of their personal and career expectations; and have provided themselves with any necessary domestic support services. Generally, decision-making within such partnerships is shared and reasonably egalitarian, even though male partners' careers will, *in the last instance,* tend to take priority. The major sources of strain surround child rearing and the determination of parental roles. Of course, dual-career couples are not new; indeed, their features have been discussed in various investigations (Rapoport and Rapoport, 1978). However, in our view, the predicted spread of dual-*career,* as opposed to dual-*occupational* couples (where both partners are employed but only one, typically the man, has a career occupation) has been greatly exaggerated. Further, for both types, we suspect that the extent to which professional and work interests spill over into private lives appears to have been overstated.

The second model of conjugal relationships bears some similarity with the conventional middle-class marriage as described by Handy (1978):

> The husband works and the wife minds the home. She wants him and the children to be happy. His achievement and success, up to a point, are her goals as well. She concentrates

her activities around the home, the husband/wife relationship, the family and their social network . . . The wife's task, as she sees it, is to absorb her own problems and those of managing the family, and not burden her husband. Within the family, his activity is channelled into conventionally defined roles and, in the husband/wife relationship, she expects him to dominate. (pp.39–40).

This description could apply to many of the couples co-operating in our own study, particularly those with children. The lifestyles and personal identities of many managers' wives, in other words, remain predominantly shaped by the constraints and demands of their husbands' jobs. Yet there are *emerging* departures from the conventional middle-class marriage pattern. It appears to be no longer true, for example, that 'the husband derives his greatest satisfaction from his job/career outside the home, while the wife derives hers, not from a job/career commitment, but from her activities within the home itself' (Gowler and Legge, 1978, pp.49–50). Indeed, as we have shown, less than one-third of the male managers in our study derive their 'greatest satisfaction' from either their jobs or their careers. Further, the 'non-career' wives of male managers are increasingly likely to seek personal satisfaction and an albeit limited sense of autonomy through obtaining part- and full-time employment. In this, they are generally encouraged by their husbands who perceive their partners' employment as improving the quality of their marital lives. At the same time, and in response to growing uncertainties, the partners of male managers are making greater attempts to protect their homes from the pressures of work. In doing so, they avoid many of the more extreme forms of occupational 'incorporation' and 'vicariousness', even though they largely remain bound by the demands of their husbands' jobs. For most women, then, remaining single or establishing careers before marriage continue to represent the most likely means of ensuring a sense of achievement and self-determination in both their private and working lives.

[177]

Notes

1 Accordingly, programmes tended to reflect the position of married women as 'homemakers' and as 'consumers' and generally reinforced prevailing notions that their primary role should be supportive to other family members.
2 As part and parcel of widespread, albeit middle-class, debate about the nature of gender roles and the extent to which family relationships repressed individual creativity.
3 This pattern was reflected within our in-depth interviews with managers' wives. Colleague-entertaining was virtually non-existent among managers employed in the public sector organizations.
4 An unintended effect of new technology which warrants more detailed research.
5 This is reinforced by a prevailing assumption that bankers' wives 'should not need to work'. Fewer of the partners of managers in the banking and financial services organization had jobs compared with the others.
6 This point was particularly emphasized by both managers and their partners in the in-depth interviews which we conducted.
7 This was especially evident among the women who were working part-time in routine clerical and lower-grade administrative positions.
8 Often causing 'crises' of personal identity and, related to these, problems in relationships with partners.

CHAPTER 8

Conclusions

We have described many of those included in our survey as 'reluctant' managers. By this, we refer to those who are less than fully committed to their jobs and who have great reservations about giving priority to their work, their careers and, indeed, their employing organizations. They are more careful, perhaps, than in the past about becoming completely 'psychologically' immersed in their occupations and seek, instead, to obtain a balance between their work and private lives. They are reluctant to strive for career success if this can be gained only at the expense of personal and family relationships. Consequently, they are less prepared to subordinate their personalities to the requirements of their work and careers. Indeed, they and their partners are increasingly inclined to resist the potentially 'greedy' demands of employing organizations as they cultivate strategies for maintaining the non-work autonomy of their homes and of personal relationships.

Such a response can be interpreted as an outcome of a number of corporate and broader social changes which have occurred in Britain over recent decades. In particular, the nature of the psychological contract between managers and their employing organizations has changed as more competitive market conditions and the need to cut costs have increased the pressures which large numbers of them now experience. Many feel that they are subject to greater demands to work harder and under more tightly monitored circumstances. Indeed, this seems to be just as much the case for those working in 'looser' as well as in more bureaucratically structured organizations. While, in the latter, behaviour is monitored according to formally prescribed rules and

[179]

procedures, in the former, performance is more characteristically stipulated through the use of predetermined targets. At the same time, many are having to achieve their tasks with limited financial resources and with 'cut-backs' in staff levels. This may require them to accomplish goals with under-qualified subordinates and, indeed, to undertake tasks for which they have had little, if any, training. As a result, large numbers of managers feel that that are subject to 'excessive' pressures and query whether the rewards are worth the effort; if their employing organizations cannot guarantee security and promotion prospects, why should they, in turn, be prepared to invest themselves *fully* in their jobs? Accordingly, they are more cautious about their commitment to employing organizations if only because of the greater risks of career 'failure', redundancy and redeployment. As a personal counter-strategy, therefore, feelings of psychological well-being can be sustained through limiting the extent of their occupational involvement and corporate attachment.

More generally, despite the resurgence of a political rhetoric which emphasizes the virtues of 'Victorian' values, many of the predominant ideals of present-day Britain do not support attitudes which give priority to work and careers (Handy, 1984; Robertson, 1985). If, in the past, there was a pronounced work ethic which fostered a desire for occupational achievement and nurtured work-based values around which personal identities could be constructed, this has now diminished. Middle-class affluence, resulting in higher levels of personal consumption, has increased the significance of non-work lifestyles and leisure patterns. Managers' personal identities, therefore, are no longer solely derived from their jobs but, instead, are also shaped by a variety of non-work factors. Indeed, those who are excessively committed to their jobs may be stigmatized as ambitious, selfish 'workaholics' because of the extent to which they are prepared to neglect their family and personal relationships (Evans and Bartolomé, 1980). 'Careerism' can often be a term of abuse and, increasingly, notions of personal success incorporate the ability to cultivate and maintain close personal relationships within networks of family, friends and acquaintances. For some, then, occupational achievements may be valued more for their *extrinsic* than their *intrinsic* rewards. Successful careers are perceived as *means* for obtaining higher levels of remuneration which, in turn, enable the enjoyment of relatively affluent lifestyles and high level of personal consumption. Promotion can be interpreted predominantly in these terms and, removed from particular organizational settings, may have limited effects for personal identity. Indeed, the maintenance of sharp distinctions between work and non-work identities serves an important function since, while 'significant others' may know little about personal occupational achievements, equally *lack* of promotion and career success can be more easily disguised. Some managers, then, underplay their career achievements and stress their 'detachment' from their jobs.[1] This can help them to cope with any real or potential threats of redundancy and with adjusting to the underachievement of goals which they may have set themselves when they were younger. Such strategies are often reinforced by relatively high earnings which enable them to engage in a variety of leisure pursuits that provide 'alternative' routes for personal achievement and self-accomplishment. In our in-depth interviews, managers often described their work and careers in detail but with limited enthusiasm; only when they discussed their leisure and home-based activities did they demonstrate any degree of excitement. Such leisure pursuits cannot simply be regarded as sources of relaxation and forms of compensation for the stresses which they experience at work. Rather, they constitute spheres of autonomy within which particular talents and skills can be nurtured for the purposes of achieving 'genuine' satisfaction and personal development. Consequently, personal priorities become structured around these various creative leisure pursuits rather than around work. Of course, many are reluctant to admit this publicly since, in their working lives, the 'demonstration' of commitment repre-

[181]

sents an important strategy for motivating staff. At work, they do what is expected of them for the purpose of achieving goals, but they frequently seem to regard their non-work roles as *personally* more salient. Of course, this creates dilemmas and contradictions and many find they must become skilful role players. The fact that some appear unable to sustain this 'performance' over protracted periods of time may account for their expressed desire to take early retirement, to 'opt out' and, sometimes, to start their own businesses (Scase and Goffee, 1987).

However, the tendency for some managers to disguise or underplay their career achievements is not only a means whereby they are better able to cope with the uncertainties of rapid organizational change. It is also a function of middle-class values which tend to regard personal 'success' with a considerable degree of *ambiguity* (Pahl and Pahl, 1971). While there is much admiration for self-made entrepreneurs and – paradoxically – for those occupying positions of power and prestige by virtue of their more privileged social origins, this is less likely to be the case for those who are successful in managerial careers. They, by contrast, can be targets for personal abuse, for having sacrificed themselves to their jobs and for being 'company slaves'. Indeed, those who do enjoy rapid promotion may find themselves removed from personal networks and colleague-based friendship groups and, as a result, socially marginalized. The operation of such interpersonal influences within large-scale organizations can inhibit the promotion ambitions of middle and junior managers, and encourage them to 'satisfize' rather than to 'optimize' (Simon, 1960).

But, of course, not *all* managers are 'reluctant'. The processes of organizational and social change which we describe have had their greatest impact amongst *middle-aged, middle-level, male* managers. There continue to be successful older, senior managers for whom occupational achievement remains a primary source of life satisfaction.[2] The working patterns and lifestyles of these individuals may differ little

[182]

from their counterparts two or three decades ago – although even here retirement ages have dropped significantly. In addition, there are some younger managers, currently on elaborately designed corporate 'fast tracks', whose exaggerated enthusiasm for work has become a distinguishing feature. These individuals, frequently MBA-educated and popularly characterized as 'yuppies', herald an important change in work attitudes. In our view, however, their small numbers suggest that the impact within large mainstream British corporations will be extremely limited over the next decade.[3] Women managers, too, as we have shown in this book, tend to display different work orientations to those of their male colleagues; certainly, more continue to see their careers as a primary source of life satisfaction. But, despite recent increases, their numbers are likely to remain limited, particularly at more senior organizational levels.

It is our contention, then, that large corporations in Britain contain within them substantial numbers of reluctant managers and, further, that this has a significant impact on corporate performance. Who, after all, ensures that the strategies formulated by top executives will actually be *implemented* if it is not these same middle managers? What, then, have those senior executives who recognize the problem done to regain the commitment of their colleagues? Several courses of action have been considered, some of which we have discussed during the course of this book. In some cases, there have been attempts to redesign jobs in ways which allow individuals to experience a greater sense of challenge and personal development in their work. As we reported in Chapter 2, many managers feel that these elements are currently lacking in their jobs and that, as a result, their organizations are not fully utilizing their skills. Generally, however, attempts at job enrichment have focused upon unskilled and semi-skilled manual employees rather than managers. The latter have more typically been given opportunities to make lateral transfers between existing jobs as a means of providing broader experience, given the existence of promotion blockages of the kind discussed in Chapter 4. (Hunt, 1984).

But there are a number of technological and organizational factors which tend to constrain the operation of such schemes and there are limits to the extent to which individuals are prepared to remove themselves periodically to functions where they may have little competence and no experience. Indeed, unless these schemes are set within a comprehensive programme of training and development, there is an inevitable tendency for managers to regard transfer as a poor substitute for promotion. Managers' anxieties about their own competences may, of course, be addressed through various kinds of educational and skills training programmes. As we discussed in Chapter 3, most managers feel that training in human relations skills should be a major input within such programmes. Many feel, for example, that their abilities to influence, to delegate, and to lead teams are inadequate and increasingly exposed within the more performance-driven climate of the 1980s. Yet, as several recent reports have demonstrated, the level of management development and training within most companies is derisory; indeed, a substantial proportion of British managers receive no 'off-the-job' training whatsoever (Constable and McCormick, 1987; Handy, 1987). Given increasing requirements for 'skill transferability', 'flexibility' and 'adaptability', the lack of resources devoted to management training suggests an absence of any kind of long-term human resource perspective at senior levels within many large organizations.

The emphasis upon short-term results is perhaps best illustrated by the current popularity of performance-related pay systems. These are seen as a means by which managers may be 'remotivated', given the declining impact of appeals to corporate 'loyalty' and 'duty'. By linking individual rewards more closely to measurable outputs, so it is claimed, managers, like any other employees, can be encouraged to expand greater effort – at least in the short-term. In practice, however, such schemes can falter if, as is the case in many

[184]

management jobs, individual performance is difficult to measure and, indeed, almost impossible to separate from the efforts of colleagues. There is the added danger, as we discussed in Chapter 2, that attempts to break managerial jobs down into a series of measurable targets can eliminate a sense of challenge and, thereby, demotivate managers.

A longer-term perspective has been taken by those senior corporate managers who have deliberately attempted to create strong corporate-based values and ideals as a means by which managerial effort can be harnessed collectively (Goldsmith and Clutterbuck, 1984). More than any other approach, perhaps, this represents a deliberate counter-strategy to the tendency for a growing number of managers to define their employment primarily in calculative and instrumental ways. This is an attempt, in other words, to tie managers into a set of all-embracing ideals and 'missionary' aims which go well beyond the mundane objectives of, on the one hand, individuals to earn a living and, on the other, corporations to make a profit. For these reasons, senior managers now place considerable emphasis upon the development of appropriate 'leadership styles' which personally reflect corporate goals and ideals and offer direction to others. As we have argued earlier in this book, the practical difficulties of introducing such ideas, particularly within large, diversified multinationals, which have grown largely by acquisition, are enormous. But there are further, more intractable problems which derive from the broader nature of *British* culture. For various historical reasons, qualities of 'leadership' in Britain have traditionally been associated with specific characteristics. The public schools, the military and the higher echelons of the civil service have shaped what have become regarded as the necessary behavioural characteristics of those in positions of authority (Weiner, 1981). Particular patterns of conduct are required in terms of speech, dress and personal appearance. It is, then, assumed that certain core values, attitudes and beliefs are adhered to. Leadership 'skills', therefore, may be difficult to acquire, if only because they are derived through particular child rearing patterns, education and class-based experiences. The persistence of such styles results from the tendency for senior managers to recruit successors with similar personal characteristics. Such processes militate against the career opportunities of those from working-class origins, of women and of others who have been unable to acquire the intangible but *real* personal attributes of class privilege.[4] As a result, highly competent managers may be excluded from top-level corporate-based networks because of their lack of acceptable personal skills. Such disadvantages in career terms can only be overcome through various forms of patronage, but ambitious and talented managers may not be sponsored precisely because they are seen to lack these 'necessary' attributes. Those who are chosen often endure heavy personal costs as they try to emulate the interpersonal styles of senior executives. This can lead to the breakup of personal relationships and heightened feelings of social marginality. Rejected by close colleagues and yet not fully accepted by those in higher positions, ambitious middle managers can be confronted with severe identity problems.

The source of many of these dilemmas, found as they are within many large-scale organizations, can be traced, in part at least, to persisting class divisions within British society.[5] Arguments which claim that the effectiveness of companies can only be achieved by improving the competence of managers through enhancing specialist and technical skills are, to some extent, missing the point. Whilst the performance of business corporations is likely to be improved if managers are highly motivated and prepared to commit themselves wholeheartedly to the attainment of corporate goals, the perpetuation of particular assumptions amongst senior management, emphasizing the 'natural superiority' of particular leadership skills, can 'exclude' talented individuals and inhibit their corporate ambitions. In this context policies designed to improve the quantity and quality of management training may have limited impact. Indeed, they could exacerbate tensions which already exist within many organizations

[186]

through the co-existence of meritocratic and more traditional values related to social class. As managers become better trained and technically more qualified for their jobs, they could become more disaffected as they recognize that such skills are not always valued as highly as those derived from particular privileged home and educational experiences. If, then, the hidden dimensions of class are expressed in interpersonal relationships within management hierarchies, it is not entirely surprising that many British companies, in comparison with international competitors, devote relatively few resources to human resource management and to the career development of their employees. In other societies, by contrast, the absence of acute, class-related differences in personal relationships and interpersonal skills assists companies in their attempts to develop more 'open', meritocratic methods of personal assessment and, as a result, to nurture career strategies for their managers.

It is for such reasons that we doubt whether strategies to create corporate 'excellence' through identifying 'core' values, to which all managers subscribe – irrespective of their functional and technical skills – can be widely successful in Britain. In a society with pronounced divisions, social cleavages will be reflected in corporate structures and, as a result, will limit how far particular and specific 'core' values can integrate the energies of all employees. The structural features of large organizations both generate and reflect class differences in the wider society (Salaman, 1981). This is most evident in disputes over payment systems, productivity and staffing levels. But it is also expressed in general feelings of employee resentment and in the persistence of *low trust* at various organizational levels, including management (Fox, 1974). Thus, although managers are rarely engaged in overt disputes with their companies, they are often resentful about their remuneration, conditions of service and promotion opportunities. Such feelings tend to be reflected in their failure to exercise 'initiative', their low motivation and limited employer commitment. The existence of low levels of inter-

[187]

personal trust sustains among managers cautious attitudes towards colleagues, subordinates and immediate bosses. These are particularly noticeable within large traditional manufacturing enterprises where there are highly visible divisions of interest between managers and productive employees (Beynon 1983; Nichols and Beynon, 1977). The possible exception may be those smaller firms where the technical skills and earnings of employers and employees are much the same (Goffee and Scase, 1982). By contrast, authority relationships in large organizations tend to reflect wider social divisions and militate against the imposition of 'shared values'. This is, perhaps most clearly recognized by those managers who emphasize their 'right to manage'; they are aware of the nature of power relationships within large organizations and remain largely sceptical of those who try to improve employee motivation through appeals which emphasize consensus and common values.

If this is the case, what are the strategies that senior managers can adopt for improving the operating performance of their companies? It is our view that although more fashionable 'adhocratic' and 'loose-knit' forms of organization may be appropriate in, for example, such areas as 'high' technology, electronics, advertising, public relations and media production, most large-scale corporations will continue to depend upon predominantly bureaucratic means for attaining goals. Beyond the 'technical' advantages of organizing in this way in order to deliver, on a large scale, standardized products and services, there are significant 'cultural' supports for the bureaucratic form. Broader social divisions in British society tend to generate low-trust relationships and bring about a dependency upon rules and regulations which are, themselves, sources of conflict and interpersonal friction. At the same time, the higher-educational system in Britain fosters psychological 'compliance' and 'conformity' rather than 'creativity' among those who are likely to become future managers.[6] Thus, it becomes a commonly held belief among senior managers that their

[188]

more junior colleagues *expect* 'tight' systems of control and are actually attracted by bureaucratized forms of organization. Although managers may regularly complain of 'red tape' and 'unnecessary' rules and procedures, they will, at the same time, emphasize the need for detailed job descriptions and precise measures of operating performance. Thus, many large organizations become 'rule-bound' and non-adaptive to change.

The bureaucratic model appears, then, to be compatible with broader social processes as these are associated with the educational system and the predominant cultural values of British society. As such, the applicability of rather 'looser' organizational forms, integrated by senior-management appeals to 'shared ideals' and characterized by flexible, 'adhocratic' working practices, is likely to be pertinent for only a limited range of organizational settings. Rules, clearly defined procedures and hierarchical authority will continue to form the basis for the exercise of managerial prerogatives in work contexts in which personal relationships, particularly those between superordinates and subordinates, are characterized by low trust. Accordingly, the performance of many large companies in Britain is unlikely to improve unless their predominant management style can be changed. Indeed, there are severe limitations in the extent to which this can be accomplished in view of the pervading influence of broader social factors. Even so, it is, perhaps, significant that many large corporations have been 'turned around' and restructured in Britain by appointing chief executives from abroad. They have often proceeded to impose predominant management styles which are less rule-bound and which encourage innovation and creativity.[7] Japanese-owned companies operating in Britain have also introduced 'new' work practices, but although such changes have been generally successful in improving productivity, it is uncertain whether this can be sustained over a longer term as, perhaps inevitably, broader social influences permeate work settings (White and Trevor, 1983). These, however, are very atypical circumstances and, on the whole, the motivation and commitment of many middle managers to their employing organizations would seem to be low. An increase in the provision and quality of management education and training may improve their technical and conceptual competences but, as we have stated, this could also heighten their feelings of disaffection unless there are more fundamental changes in the prevailing assumptions and values of many large organizations. However, there is some evidence that one category of managers, detached from these prevailing ideals, could be an important source of innovation. These are the increasing numbers of women who are predominantly 'locked' into junior and middle-level positions. For many, as we have shown, their jobs and careers are the major priorities in their lives. Further, their disengagement from the predominant male-based managerial practices could enable them to become a major force for revitalizing the performance of large organizations in the 1990s; witness, for instance, their successes in the United States and their achievements as entrepreneurs in Britain (Goffee and Scase, 1985). In these ventures, they are often able to achieve high rates of business growth by motivating their employees through developing innovative styles of management.

In the meantime, it is likely that many managers will not be strongly committed to their jobs and, instead, will develop their talents and establish 'life priorities' in various non-work spheres. They will, as a result, see their employment primarily as a source of income for the purpose of nurturing such identities and lifestyles. In this, they are likely to be encouraged by their spouses to distance themselves from their jobs and to maintain sharp psychological barriers between home and work. With such partially committed managers, senior executives may be forced to rely upon bureaucratic forms of organization, within what are essentially 'low trust' work settings, for the purposes of achieving corporate goals. Such organizations are likely to be fairly rigid in their operating procedures and, as a result, insufficiently adaptive

[190]

to changing market circumstances. A number of corporations may succeed in cultivating 'cultures of excellence' and introducing more flexible organizational forms, but predominant practice in Britain will tend, we suspect, to lead mainly to the *compliance* of reluctant managers.

Notes

1 This was particularly noticeable in our in-depth interviews which were conducted in the respondents' homes. Some individuals seemed almost to exaggerate the extent to which they psychologically and emotionally distanced themselves from their jobs.

2 This, of course, is almost true by definition because of the nature of promotion processes as related to appointments to senior managerial positions.

3 We suspect that their presence is more evident within the popular media than in the offices of large-scale corporations.

4 Patterns of working–class recruitment into senior managerial and professional positions in Britain are notoriously low. Any fluidity within the class structure tends to be between working-class and lower middle–class occupations. See Goldthorpe (1980). Not surprisingly, in our own study the educational and social backgrounds of senior managers reflected these broader patterns. Seven in ten had fathers who were employed in professional, managerial and administrative occupations (by comparison to four in ten for other managers); one in four had a public school education (by contrast with one in seven other managers).

5 In the extent to which class relationships have important ramifications for the structuring of personal identities and, hence, the nature of interpersonal skills.

6 Primarily because 'élite' institutions which have provided models for the development of higher education in general, have traditionally met the needs of the independent professions and the higher echelons of the Civil Service.

7 However, attempts to encourage innovation appear unlikely to succeed if a climate of insecurity and uncertainty persists. 'Turnaround' managers are often succeeded by others who are better able to foster a sense of security amongst employees.

[191]

Methodological appendix

The findings presented in this book are derived from a survey of 374 managers, of whom 323 are men and 51 women.[1] They were asked to complete questionnaires, consisting of both precoded and open-ended questions.[2] These were distributed to managers at their place of work and completed in the presence of the investigators. This enabled us to obtain a response rate of almost 100 per cent. All those taking part were assured of complete confidentiality, both in terms of their own identities and those of their employing organizations. From the original survey of managers, a representative group of eighty men and women were selected for further in-depth interviews. These were loosely structured, relying upon open-ended questions and focusing around a number of 'key' themes. All of the eighty interviews were undertaken in the respondents' homes, tape recorded and later transcribed. These were conducted in the presence of husbands, wives or partners (where applicable) who were also asked a number of questions during the interview sessions.

The managers are employed in six large organizations based in the United Kingdom. Four of these are privately owned but publicly quoted companies, while two are in the public sector. The organizations were chosen so as to reflect different sectors of the economy and within which substantial numbers of managers are employed. Accordingly, they were selected so as to be indicative of trends in (i) 'traditional' forms of industrial manufacturing; (ii) 'high' electronic technology engineering; (iii) large-scale banking and financial

[192]

services; (iv) hotel, tourism and personal services; (v) the provision of 'standardized' public sector utilities; and (vi) the public sector provision of education, health and social welfare services. All of the privately owned corporations are 'household names', with each of them having more than 50,000 employees. They are in the 'top fifty' of British companies as assessed by their quoted market value on the London Stock Exchange. The public utility corporation also employs more than 50,000 staff while the remaining public sector organization has a payroll of over 20,000.

The managers, then, are employed within very large organizations, each of which operates within a different sector of the economy, utilizing a variety of technological and work processes. However, each of the organizations is structured according to various forms of divisionalization. This, therefore, shapes the allocation of budgets, the assessment of operating and financial performance as well as, of course, the nature of career paths available to managers. But despite their common divisionalized characteristics, there are many differences between the six organizations in terms of their operating practices. Some are attempting to break down departmental rigidities through creating interdepartmental 'project teams', while others are trying to extend financial and operating autonomy to divisional units. All of the six organizations are confronted with *internal* and *external* changes. As a result, like many large British corporations, they are undergoing processes of restructuring, both in terms of their decision-making processes and their management systems. Indeed, it is for such reasons that we chose managers from these organizations.

In our selection of managers for the questionnaire survey we tried to obtain a broad spread of age groups chosen from different functional specialisms within each of the six organizations. In line with Labour Force Survey (1985) data, the highest proportion of the male managers in our study are middle-aged, concentrated within the 35–44 age range. Women managers, by contrast, are younger, partly because of their more recent entry into managerial positions and also because of the particular nature of their careers; many choose or are forced to disrupt their careers in their late 20s and early 30s. The age distribution of the men and women taking part in our study is as follows:

Table A1 Percentage Distribution of Respondents According to Their Age

Age categories	Men (N = 324)	Women (N = 51)
Under 25	0	0
25 – 34	26	49
35 – 44	44	31
45 – 54	26	18
55 and over	4	2
	100	100

A substantial proportion of both men and women in our study describe themselves as 'general managers'; 29 per cent and 22 per cent respectively. This may seem high but it is, in fact, comparable with figures obtained in recent surveys conducted by the British Institute of Management (Alban-Metcalfe and Nicholson, 1984). The women are more likely to be engaged in 'personnel, training and industrial relations' whereas none of them are engaged in production management. Again this reflects broader labour market patterns rather than peculiarities in our study. The overall distribution of respondents among different functional specialisms is given in Table A2.

For the purpose of the study, these managers were coded into three categories of responsibility – senior, middle and junior. This was undertaken on the basis of information provided by respondents and their employing organizations, taking into account such factors as job titles, salaries, descriptions of their day-to-day work tasks and their responsibilities for financial, capital and human resources. Their distribution in terms of seniority is shown in Table A3.

[194]

Table A2 Percentage Distribution of Respondents in Terms of Functional Groupings

Stated functional specialism	Men (N = 324)	Women (N = 51)
General Management	29	22
Production	10	none
Sales and Marketing	12	6
Finance and Accounting	16	16
Research and Development	1	2
Engineering and Maintenance	6	8
Personnel, Training and Industrial Relations	5	22
Administration	14	12
Other	7	12
	100	100

Table A3 Percentage Distribution of Respondents in Terms of their Positions of Seniority

	Men (N = 324)	Women (N = 51)
Senior	23	2
Middle	42	36
Junior	35	62
	100	100

By comparison with their distribution within the economy as a whole, our study is 'skewed' towards *middle* and, to a lesser extent, *senior* managers. Thus, Constable and McCormick (1987) estimate that nationally 13 per cent of managers are found in senior, 29 per cent in middle and 58 per cent in junior positions. As Table A3 also shows, women are concentrated in the study, as nationally, within junior managerial positions.

Managers are relatively well-paid by comparison with other groups within the occupational structure. In terms of our own study, the overall distribution of their earnings is comparable with the trends identified in salary surveys conducted by the British Institute of Management. As a reflection of differences in their organizational positions and functional specialisms, women tend to be paid less than men. Whereas 20 per cent of the men earn in excess of £20,000 per annum, this is the case for only 2 per cent of women. Table A4 give details of their gross earnings but excludes information about their rewards in terms of a variety of fringe benefits (see Chapter 2).

Table A4 Percentage Distribution of Respondents' Gross Annual Earnings

Gross Annual Earnings (£)	Men (N = 324)	Women (N = 51)
25,000+	6	none
20 – 25,000	14	2
15 – 20,000	32	37
10 – 15,000	42	53
Below 10,000	6	8
	100	100

Ninety-two per cent of the men and 80 per cent of the women reported they had been in continuous employment since completing their full-time education. The contrast between men and women is to be expected, given the greater likelihood of their careers being interrupted by a variety of circumstances (see Chapter 4). However, the fact that as many as four-fifths of the female respondents have been in continuous employment reflects their younger age as indicated in Table A1. In terms of their employing organizations, roughly one-third of both men and women had worked for only one employer during the whole of their working lives, while a further one-third had worked for four or more. Their distribution is shown in Table A5.

If there are differences between the men and women in our study in terms of their salaries and positions of responsibility, these are reinforced by contrasts in the level of their educational qualifications and their marital status. Whereas 37 per

Table A5 Percentage Distribution of Respondents According to their Employment Experiences

Nos of employing organizations	Men (N = 324)	Women (N = 51)
Only one	35	29
2 – 3	38	38
4 or more	27	33

cent of the women had *at least* university degrees, this was the case for only 22 per cent of the men. To some extent, of course, this reflects their younger age and the changing labour market circumstances of recent years. It also indicates an increasing recognition among senior management that those who are recruited for their managerial potential should be university graduates. The higher qualifications of these younger women in our own study does, in fact, fit with the findings of other studies and is in line with broader trends (Nicholson and West, 1988).

Women managers tend not only to be younger than their male colleagues, but are also less likely to be married. So it is with the respondents in our own study. Whereas 93 per cent of the men are either married or living with a partner, this is the case for 55 per cent of the women. Only 3 per cent of the former have never been married or lived with a partner compared with 35 per cent of the women respondents.

Overall, we make no claim that the men and women taking part in our study constitute a *representative sample;* they are selected from only six, albeit very large, employing organizations. It is for this reason that there are no statistical tests of significance in the analysis of the data which we present throughout our discussion. At best, our findings can only be regarded as *indicative* of broader trends as these are affecting the work, careers and personal experiences of men and women managers during the closing decades of the twentieth century. For reasons to do with constraints of both time and finance, it was not possible to undertake a more comprehensive study consisting of large numbers of mana-

[197]

gers chosen from a wider range of employment experiences. In some ways, investigations of this sort are already undertaken in the regular surveys conducted by the British Institute of Management. However, by comparison with more academically oriented studies, the present research is relatively ambitious in terms of its scale. It compares favourably, for instance, with the influential studies of Pahl and Pahl (1971), and of Sofer (1970); in the research of the former, 86 male managers were interviewed, while, in the latter, there were 81 male managers selected from only two companies. Thus, without any statistical claims to representativeness, we would hope that our research offers a relevant description of present-day patterns and suggests some pointers as to future trends.

Notes

1   The relative proportions of men and women were chosen so as to reflect those within the wider management population.
2   Unfortunately, for reasons of space, the questionnaire is not reproduced in this book. Details are available from the authors. Our use of questions which are identical or similar to those used in earlier studies – for example, Pahl and Pahl (1971); Poole, *et al.* (1981); Evans and Bartolomé (1980) – represents a deliberate attempt to compare our findings with those collected in earlier periods.

Bibliography

Abrams, P. and McCulloch, A. (1976), *Communes, Sociology and Society* (Cambridge: Cambridge University Press).

Alban-Metcalfe, B. and Nicholson, N. (1984), *The Career Development of British Managers* (London: British Institute of Management).

Aron, R. (1967), *The Industrial Society* (London: Weidenfeld & Nicholson).

Bamber, L. (1976), 'Trade unions for managers', *Personnel Review*, vol. 5.

Bannock, G. (1987), *Britain in the 1980s: Enterprise Reborn?* (London: Investors in Industry).

Barnard, C. (1938), *The Functions of the Executive* (Cambridge, Mass.: Harvard University Press).

Bartol, K. M. (1980), 'Female managers and the quality of working life: the impact of sex-role stereotypes', *Journal of Occupational Behaviour*, vol. 1.

Belbin, R. (1981), *Management Teams: Why They Succeed or Fail* (London: Heinemann).

Bell, C. (1968), *Middle Class Families* (London: Routledge & Kegan Paul).

Bell, D. (1974), *The Coming of Post-Industrial Society* (London: Heinemann).

Berthoud, R. (1979), *Unemployed Professionals and Executives* (London: Policy Studies Institute).

Beynon, H. (1983), *Working for Ford,* 2nd edn (Harmondsworth: Penguin).

Boddy, D. and Buchanan D. (1986), *Managing New Technology* (Oxford: Blackwell).

Bott, E. (1957), *Family and Social Network* (London: Tavistock).

Bowey, A. M. (1982), *Handbook of Salary and Wage Systems,* 2nd edn (Aldershot: Gower).

Brake, M. (1985), *Comparative Youth Culture* (London: Routledge & Kegan Paul).

[199]

Braverman, H. (1974), *Labor and Monopoly Capital* (New York: Monthly Review Press).

British Institute of Management (1985), *National Management Salary Survey* (Corby: British Institute of Management).

Brown, R. (1982), 'Work histories, career structures and class structure', in A. Giddens and G. Mackenzie (eds), *Social Class and the Division of Labour* (Cambridge: Cambridge University Press).

Bryman, A. (1986), *Leadership and Organizations* (London: Routledge & Kegan Paul).

Buchanan, D. and Boddy, D. (1983), *Organizations in the Computer Age: Technological Imperatives and Strategic Choice* (Aldershot: Gower).

Burns, T. and Stalker, G. (1961), *The Management of Innovation* (London: Tavistock).

Carchedi, G. (1975), 'On the economic identification of the new middle class', *Economy and Society,* vol. 4.

Carlson, S. (1951), *Executive Behaviour: a Study of the Workload and Working Methods of Managing Directors* (Stockholm: Strobergs).

Carter, R. (1985), *Capitalism, Class Conflict and the New Middle Class* (London: Routledge & Kegan Paul).

Child, J. (1984), *Organization,* 2nd edn (New York: Harper & Row).

Clutterbuck, D. and Devine, M. (1987), 'Having a mentor: A help or a hindrance', in D. Clutterbuck and M. Devine (eds), *Businesswoman: Present and Future* (Basingstoke: Macmillan).

Cohen, G. (1977), 'Absentee husbands in spiralist families: the myth of the symmetrical family', *Journal of Marriage and the Family,* vol. 39.

Constable, J. and McCormick, R. (1987), *The Making of British Managers: A Report for the BIM and the CBI into Management Training, Education and Development* (Corby: British Institute of Management).

Cooper, C. (1980), *The Stress Check: Coping with Life and Work Stress* (Englewood Cliffs, NJ: Prentice-Hall).

Cooper, C. (1982), *Executive Families Under Stress* (Englewood Cliffs, NJ: Prentice-Hall).

Cooper, C. L. and Davidson, M. (1982), *High Pressure* (London: Fontana).

Cooper, C. L. and Marshall, J. (1978a), 'Sources of managerial and white collar stress' in C. L. Cooper and R. Payne (eds), *Stress at Work,* (Chichester: Wiley).

[200]

Cooper, C. L. and Marshall, J. (1978b), *Understanding Executive Stress* (London: Macmillan).

Crompton, R. and Sanderson, K. (1986), 'Credentials and careers: some implications of the increase in professional qualifications amongst women', *Sociology,* vol. 20, no. 1.

Crouch, C. (1977), *Class, Conflict and the Industrial Relations Crisis* (London; Heinemann).

Dahrendorf, R. (1959), *Class and Class Conflict in Industrial Society* (London: Routledge & Kegan Paul).

Davidson, M. and Cooper, C. (1983), *Stress and the Woman Manager* (Oxford: Martin Robertson).

Davis, H. and Scase, R. (1985), *Western Capitalism and State Socialism* (Oxford: Blackwell).

Department of Employment (1985), *New Earnings Survey* (London: HMSO).

Dickson, D. (1974), *Alternative Technology and the Politics of Technical Change* (London: Fontana).

Drucker, P. (1974), *Management: Tasks, Responsibilities and Practices* (London: Heinmann).

Dunnell, K. (1979), *Family Formation* (London: Office of Population Censuses and Surveys).

Edgell, S. (1980), *Middle-Class Couples* (London: Allen & Unwin).

Elliott, B. and McCrone D. (1987), 'Class culture and morality: a sociological analysis of the New Conservatism', *Sociological Review,* vol. 35.

Ellul, J. (1975), *The Technological Society* (London: Jonathan Cape).

Eurostat (1981), *The Economic and Social Position of Women in the Community* (Luxembourg: European Economic Community).

Evans, P. and Bartolomé, F. (1980), *Must Success Cost So Much?* (London: Grant McIntyre).

Fayol, H. (1949), *General and Industrial Management* (Boston: Pitman).

Fielder, F. and Chemers, M. (1974), *Leadership and Effective Management* (Glenview, Ill.: Scott Foreman).

Finch, J. (1983), *Married to the Job* (London: Allen & Unwin).

Fineman, S. (1983), *White-Collar Unemployment: Impact and Stress* (Chichester: Wiley).

Forester, T. (1987), *High-Tech Society* (Oxford: Blackwell).

Fox, A. (1974), *Beyond Contract: Work, Power and Trust Relations* (London: Faber).

Francis, A. (1986), *New Technology at Work* (Oxford: Oxford University Press).

French, J. R. P. and Caplan, R. D. (1973), 'Organizational stress and individual strain', in A. J. Marrow (ed.), *The Failure of Success* (New York: AMACOM).

Galbraith, J. (1967), *The New Industrial State* (Harmondsworth: Penguin).

Gallie, D. (1978), *In Search of the New Working Class* (Cambridge: Cambridge University Press).

Gans, H. J. (1967), *The Levittowners* (London: Allen Lane).

Gavron, H. (1968). *The Captive Wife* (Harmondsworth: Penguin).

Glaser, B. and Strauss, A. (1971), *Status Passage* (London: Routledge & Kegan Paul).

Goffee, R. (1976), 'Kent miners: stability and change in work and community', PhD thesis, University of Kent.

Goffee, R. and Scase, R. (1982), 'Fraternalism and paternalism as employer strategies in small firms', in G. Day (ed.), *Diversity and Decomposition in the Labour Market* (Aldershot: Gower).

Goffee, R. and Scase, R. (1985a), *Women in Charge* (London: Allen & Unwin).

Goffee, R. and Scase, R. (1985b), 'Women in management – where now?' *London Business School Journal,* vol. 6, no. 2.

Goffee, R. and Scase, R. (1986), 'Are the rewards worth the effort? Changing managerial values in the 1980s', *Personnel Review,* vol. 15, no. 4.

Goffman, E. (1959), *The Presentation of Self in Everyday Life* (Garden City, NJ: Anchor).

Goldthorpe, J. (1984), 'The end of convergence; corporatist and dualist tendencies in modern western societies', in J. Goldthorpe (ed.), *Order and Conflict in Contemporary Capitalism* (Oxford: Oxford University Press).

Goldthorpe, J. H. (1980), *Social Mobility and Class Structure in Modern Britain* (Oxford: Clarendon).

Goldthorpe, J. H., Lockwood, D., Bechhofer, F. and Platt, J. (1969), *The Affluent Worker in the Class Structure* (Cambridge: Cambridge University Press).

Goldsmith, W. and Clutterbuck, D. (1984), *The Winning Streak* (London: Weidenfeld & Nicolson).

Gorz, A. (1982), *Farewell to the Working Class* (London: Pluto Press).

Gospel, H. (1978), 'European managerial unions: an early assessment', *Industrial Relations,* vol. 17.

Gouldner, A. (1954), *Patterns of Industrial Bureaucracy* (Glencoe, Ill.: Free Press).

Gowler, D. and Legge, K. (1978), 'Hidden and open contracts in marriage', in R. Rapoport and R. Rapoport (eds), *Working Couples* (London: Allen & Unwin).

Gowler, D. and Legge, K. (1982), 'Dual worker families', in R. Rapoport, M. Fogarty and R. Rapoport (eds), *Families in Britain* (London: Routledge & Kegan Paul).

Guerrier, Y. and Philpott, N. (1978), *The British Manager: Careers and Mobility* (London: British Institute of Management).

Gutek, B., Nakamura, C. U. and Nieva, B. G. (1981), 'The interdependence of work and family roles', *Journal of Occupational Behaviour,* vol. 2, no. 1.

Hall, D. T. (1976), *Careers in Organisations* (Santa Monica, Calif.: Goodyear).

Handy, C. (1978), 'Going against the grain: working couples and greedy occupations', in R. Rapoport and R. Rapoport (eds), *Working Couples* (London: Allen & Unwin).

Handy, C. (1983), *Taking Stock: Being Fifty in The Eighties* (London: BBC Publications).

Handy, C. (1984), *The Future of Work* (Oxford: Blackwell).

Handy, C. (1985), *Gods of Management* (London: Pan).

Handy, C. (1987), *The Making of Managers: a Report on Management Education, Training and Development in the USA, West Germany, France, Japan and the UK* (London: National Economic Development Office).

Hannah, L. (1975), *The Rise of the Corporate Economy* (London: Methuen).

Hannah, L. and Kay, J. (1977), *Concentration in Modern Industry* (London: Macmillan).

Harrison, R. (1972), 'How to describe your organization', *Harvard Business Review* (September–October).

Hearn, J. (1977), 'Towards a concept of non-career', *Sociological Review,* vol. 25.

Hennig, M. and Jardim, A. (1979), *The Managerial Woman* (London: Pan).

Herzberg, F., Mausner, B. and Snyderman, B. (1959), *The Motivation to Work* (New York: Wiley).

Hunt, J. W. (1984), *Management Resources: Present Problems and*

[203]

Future Trends (London: London Business School/Egon Zehnder International).

Hunt, J. W. (1986), *Managing People at Work,* 2nd edn (London: McGraw Hill).

Hunt, J. W. and Collins, R. (1983), *Managers in Mid Career Crisis* (Sydney: Wellington Lane).

Hunt, J., Lees, S., Grumbar, J. and Vivian, P. (1987), *Acquisitions – The Human Factor* (London: London Business School/Egon Zehnder International.

Hyman, R. (1972), *Strikes* (London: Fontana).

Illich, I. (1975), *Tools for Conviviality* (London: Fontana).

Jackson, M. P. (1974), *The Price of Coal* (London: Croom Helm).

Jarrett, D. (1982), *The Electronic Office* (Aldershot: Gower).

Jay, A. (1967), *Management and Machiavelli* (London: Hodder & Stoughton).

Jenkins, C. and Sherman, B. (1979), *The Collapse of Work* (London: Eyre Methuen).

Jessop, B. (1980), 'The transformation of the state in post-war Britain', in R. Scase, (ed.) *The State in Western Europe* (London: Croom Helm).

Johnson, G. and Scholes, K. (1984), *Exploring Corporate Strategy* (Englewood Cliffs, NJ: Prentice-Hall).

Kanter, R. M. (1977), *Men and Women of the Corporation* (New York: Basil Books).

Kanter, R. M. (1983), *The Change Masters* (London: Allen & Unwin).

King, R. and Nugent, N. (1979) (eds), *Respectable Rebels,* (London: Hodder & Stoughton).

Kolodny, H. (1981), 'Managing in a matrix', *Business Horizons,* March.

Kotter, J. P. (1982), *The General Managers* (London: Macmillan).

Kumar, K. (1989), 'Divisions and crisis in industrial capitalism', in R. Scase (ed.), *Industrial Societies: Crisis and Division in Western Capitalism and State Socialism* (London: Unwin Hyman).

LaRouche, J. and Ryan, R. (1984), *Strategies for Women at Work* (London: Allen & Unwin).

Larwood, L. and Wood, M. M. (1977), *Women in Management* (London: Lexington).

Leisure Consultants, (1986), *Leisure Forecasts* (Sudbury: Leisure Consultants).

Lipset, S. M. and Bendix, R. (1959), *Social Mobility in Industrial Society* (London: Heinemann).

Litwak, E. (1961), 'Occupational mobility and extended family cohesion', *American Sociological Review*, vol. 26.

McCrone, D., Elliott, B. and Bechhofer, F. (1989), 'Corporation and the New Right', in R. Scase (ed.), *Industrial Societies: Crisis and Division in Western Capitalism and State Socialism* (London: Allen & Unwin).

McGoldrick, A. (1983), 'Company early retirement schemes and private pension scheme options', *Leisure Studies*, vol. 2.

McMichael, A. J. (1978), 'Personality, behavioural and situational modifiers of work stressors', in C. C. Cooper and R. Payne (eds), *Stress at Work* (Chichester: Wiley).

Macrae, N. (1982), 'Intrapreneurial now', *Economist*, 17 April.

Mangham, I. L. (1986), *Power and Performance in Organisations* (Oxford: Blackwell).

Mansfield, R., Poole, M., Blyton, P. and Frost, P. (1981), *The British Manager in Profile* (London: British Institute of Management).

Marcuse, H. (1968), *One Dimensional Man* (London: Routledge).

Marshall, J. (1984), *Women Managers: Travellers in a Male World* (Chichester: Wiley).

Maslow, A. H. (1954), *Motivation and Personality* (New York: Harper & Row).

Merton, R. K. (1964), *Social Theory and Social Structure* (Glencoe, Ill.: Free Press).

Mills, C. W. (1951), *White Collar* (New York: Oxford University Press).

Minkes, A. (1987), *The Entrepreneurial Manager* (Harmondsworth: Penguin).

Mintzberg, H. (1973), *The Nature of Managerial Work* (Englewood Cliffs, NJ: Prentice-Hall).

Mintzberg, H. (1979), *The Structuring of Organizations* (Englewood Cliffs, NJ: Prentice-Hall).

Mitchell, J. (1971), *Women's Estate* (Harmondsworth: Penguin).

Morgan, G. (1986), *Images of Organisation* (London: Sage).

Morse, N. C. and Weiss, R. S. (1955), 'The function and meaning of work and the job', *American Sociological Review*, vol. 20.

[205]

Nichols, T. and Beynon, H. (1977), *Living with Capitalism* (London: Routledge & Kegan Paul).

Nicholson, N. and West, M. (1988), *Managerial Job Chance: Men and Women in Transition* (Cambridge: Cambridge University Press).

Oakley, A. (1982), *Subject Women* (London: Fontana).

Office of Population Censuses and Surveys (1985), *Labour Force Survey 1985* (London: HMSO).

Pahl, J. M. and Pahl, R. E. (1971), *Managers and Their Wives* (Harmondsworth: Penguin).

Pahl, R. E. (1984), *Divisions of Labour* (Oxford: Blackwell).

Parker, S. (1971), *The Future of Work and Leisure* (London: McGibbon & Kee).

Parker, S. (1983), *Leisure and Work* (London: Allen & Unwin).

Parker, S. (1986), 'Leisure', in R. Burgess (ed.), *Key Variables in Social Investigation* (London: Routledge & Kegan Paul).

Parkin, F. (1971), *Class, Inequality and Political Order* (London: MacGibbon & Kee).

Parsons, T. (1964), *The Social System* (Glencoe, Ill.: Free Press).

Pascale, R. (1985), 'The paradox of corporate culture: reconciling ourselves to socialization', *Californian Management Review,* vol. 27, no. 2.

Pascale, R. and Athos, A. (1982), *The Art of Japanese Management* (Harmondsworth: Penguin).

Peters, T. (1988), *Thriving on Chaos* (London: Macmillan).

Peters, T. and Waterman, R. (1982), *In Search of Excellence* (New York: Harper & Row).

Petty, M. and Bruning, N. (1980), 'A comparison of the relationship between subordinates, perceptions of supervisory behaviour and measures of subordinates' job satisfaction for male and female leaders', *Academy of Management Journal,* vol. 23.

Pinchot, G. (1985), *Intrapreneuring* (New York: Harper & Row).

Poole, M., Mansfield, R., Beyton, P. and Frost, P. (1981), *Managers in Focus* (Aldershot: Gower).

Porter, L. W. (1961), 'Perceived satisfaction in bottom and middle management jobs', *Journal of Applied Psychology,* vol. 46.

Purcell, J. and Sissons, K. (1983), 'Strategies and practice in the management of industrial relations', in G. Bain (eds.), *Industrial Relations in Britain* (Oxford: Blackwell).

Pym, D. (1986), *The Employment Question* (London: Freedom Press).

Rapoport, R. and Rapoport, R. (1976), *Dual Career Families Re-examined* (Oxford: Martin Robertson).

Rapoport, R. and Rapoport, R. (eds) (1978), *Working Couples* (London: Routledge & Kegan Paul).

Rapoport, R. and Sierakowski, M. (1982), 'Recent social trends in family and work in Britain', *Institute of Family and Environmental Research/Policy Studies Institute* (London).

Regional Reward Surveys (1985), *Executive Performance and Rewards* (London: Regional Reward Surveys).

Reich, C. A. (1970), *The Greening of America* (Harmondsworth: Penguin).

Robertson, J. (1985), *Future Work* (Aldershot: Gower/Temple Smith).

Roskin, R. (1986), 'Corporate culture revolution: the management development imperative', *Journal of Managerial Psychology,* vol. 1 no. 2.

Rothwell, S. (1985), 'Is management a masculine role?' *Management Education and Development,* vol. 16.

Routh, G. (1980), *Occupation and Pay in Great Britain 1906–79* (2nd edn) (London).

Rozier, B. (1980), 'Motivating managers to move on', *Personnel Management,* May 1980.

Salaman, G. (1981), *Class and the Corporation* (London: Fontana).

Salaman, G. (1989), 'Employment relationship in economic recession, in R. Scase (ed.), *Industrial Societies: Crisis and Division in Western Capitalism and State Socialism* (London: Unwin Hyman).

Scase, R. (1980), 'Introduction', in R. Scase, (ed) *The State in Western Europe* (London: Croom Helm).

Scase, R. (ed.), (1980), *The State in Western Europe* (London: Croom Helm).

Scase R. and Goffee, R. (1982), *The Entrepreneurial Middle Class* (London: Croom Helm).

Scase, R. and Goffee, R. (1986), 'Why managers turn entrepreneur', *Management Today,* August.

Scase, R. and Goffee R. (1987), *The Real World of the Small Business Owner* (London: Croom Helm).

Schein, E. H. (1978), *Career Dynamics: Matching Individual and Organizational Needs* (Reading, Mass.: Addison-Wesley).

Schein, E. H. (1985), *Organizational Culture and Leadership* (London: Jossey Bass).

Scott, B. (1984), *The Robotics Revolution* (Oxford: Blackwell).

[207]

Scott, J. (1986), *Capitalist Property and Financial Power* (Hassocks: Harvester).

Seeley, J., Smith, R. A. and Loosely, E. W. (1963), *Crestwood Heights* (New York: Wiley).

Simon, H. A. (1960), *Administrative Behaviour,* 2nd edn (London: Macmillan).

Smith, V. (1988), 'Restructuring management and management restructuring: the role of managers in corporate change', in J. Rothschild and M. Wallace (eds), *Research in Politics and Society,* Vol. 3 (Greenwich: JAI Press).

Sofer, C. (1970), *Men in Mid-Career: A Study of British Managers and Technical Specialists* (Cambridge: Cambridge University Press).

Stewart, J. (1986), *The New Management of Local Government* (London: Allen & Unwin).

Stewart, R. (1982), *Choices for the Manager* (London: McGraw Hill).

Strinati, S. (1982), *Capitalism, The State and Industrial Relations* (London: Croom Helm).

Tannenbaum, R. and Schmidt, W. (1958), 'How to choose a leadership pattern', *Harvard Business Review,* vol. 36.

Taylor, F. W. (1947), *Scientific Management* (New York: Harper & Row).

Thackray, J. (1986), 'Middle management blues', *Management Today,* August.

Toffler, A. (1985), *The Adaptive Corporation* (London: Pan).

Utton, M. (1970), *Industrial Concentration* (Harmondsworth: Penguin).

Van de Vliet, A. (1988), 'Modern Woman's Place', *Management Today* (October).

Wainwright, H. (1984), 'Women and the division of labour', in P. Abrams and R. Brown (eds), *UK Society: Work, Urbanism and Inequality* (London: Weidenfeld & Nicolson).

Watson, W. (1964), 'Social mobility and social class in industrial communities', in M. Gluckman and E. Devons (eds), *Closed Systems and Open Minds* (London: Oliver & Boyd).

Webb, M. (1982), 'The labour market', in I. Reid and E. Wormauld (eds), *Sex Differences in Britain* (London: Grant McIntyre).

Weber, M. (1947), *Theory of Social and Economic Organization* (London: William Hodge).

West, J. (1982), 'Introduction', in J. West (ed.), *Work, Women and the Labour Market* (London: Routledge & Kegan Paul).

White, M. (1981), *Payment Systems in Britain* (Aldershot: Gower).

White, M. and Trevor, M. (1983), *Under Japanese Management* (London: Heinemann).

Whitley, R. and Marceau, J. (1981), *Masters of Business? Business Schools and Business Graduates in Britain and France* (London: Tavistock).

Wiener, M. (1981), *English Culture and the Decline of the Industrial Spirit* (Cambridge: Cambridge University Press).

Wilensky, H. (1961), 'Orderly Careers and Social Participation', *American Sociological Reveiw*, vol. 26.

Wood, S. (1980), 'Management reactions to job redundancy through early retirement', *Sociological Review*, vol. 28.

Wood, S. and Dey, I. (1983), *Redundancy: Case Studies in Cooperation and Conflict* (Aldershot: Gower).

Woodward, J. (1958), *Management and Technology* (London: HMSO).

Whyte, W. H. (1965), *The Organization Man* (Harmondsworth: Penguin).

Young, M. (1961), *The Rise of Meritocracy* (Harmondsworth: Penguin).

Young, M. and Willmott, P. (1973), *The Symmetrical Family: A Study of Work and Leisure in the London Region* (London: Routledge & Kegan Paul).

Zweig, F. (1961), *The Worker in an Affluent Society* (London: Heinemann).

Index

active hobbies, with other family members 149–50
administrative jobs, lower-grade, managers' wives 163
administrative tasks, routine 22, 23, 28
affluent society 5
age, job dissatisfaction and 45–7
age groups
    managers studied 193–4
    sources of life satisfaction 99–100, 101
age-related stages, personal success 80–1
assertiveness 17 n6, 65–7, 120
    women managers 135
assessment centres 105 n4
assimilation 111
automation, routine tasks 35

bankers, wives 178 n5
banking 160–1
Bartolomé, F. 132–3
behaviour, at home, managers 133–5
British Institute of Management 42, 52 n7, 196, 198
building stage, careers 81
bureaucracies 1
bureaucratic model, management 10, 54–5
bureaucratic organizations 179–80, 188–9
    hierarchical nature 89
    leadership styles 63–5
    preferred by managers 72–4
bureaucratic personalities 57
business administration, graduate training 105 n6
business colleagues, entertaining 157, 162, 178 n3
business heroes 128 n6
business start-up 103–4
businesses, own, women 126–7
buy-outs 104

capital equipment, increase in 35
career achievements
    underplaying 181
    women managers 97–8
career aspirations, reduction in 142–3
career change 103
career development 187
career failure 180
career interruption, women managers 44–5
career paths, lifelong 81
career patterns, women managers 109–11
career pursuit, personal costs 99
career success 4–5
career women, single 156
career-orientation, women managers 123–5
careerism 180
careers
    failure 93–5
    geographical mobility and 137
    lifelong 82
    middle-class 78
    reassessment 103
    review 93
    success, managers' perceptions of 87–91
    traditional managerial 79–81
    women managers 85–7
child care 157
child rearing 176
children, women managers 172–4
children's education, career moves 147, 148, 165
class divisions, British society 186–7
class relationships 191 n5
clerical jobs, managers' wives 163, 164
clerical workers 9
co-ordination, management function 21
cognitive distance, work role and self-identity 33–4

[210]

cognitive styles, bureaucratic organizations 57
commitment, factor in career success 89, 90
communication, open and informal 55, 56
communication networks, informal 90
community affairs, lack of involvement 149
community involvement, managers 160
compensation, work and non-work 132
computer-based information systems 12
computer-based monitoring systems 22
conflict, work and non-work 132
conformity, bureaucratic organizations 63–4
conjugal relationships, types of 176–7
consolidation stage, careers 81
consultation, degrees of 71
consultative leadership styles 68–70
consumption, wives as symbols of 156
contrast, women 111, 113–15
control, management function 21
corporate careers 78
corporate cultures 105 n5
corporate fast tracks 183
corporate mergers 10
corporate restructuring 9
corporate strategies 183
corporate values and ideals 185
corporations, turnaround 188–9
corporatism 7, 8
cost reduction, emphasis on 9
cost-effectiveness, organizations 9
customers 178 n1

decentralized structures, organizations 9–10, 81
decision-making 22, 28, 47
  shared 61–2
deferred gratification 105 n2
delegation 29–30, 33
dependent relatives, caring for 108
deskilling 52 n1
  managers 12
  technological change 37–8
directing, management function 21
directive leadership styles 68–70

divorce rates 15
domestic help 172, 173
domestic life, separation from work 174–5
domestic relationships, women managers 170–1
domestic role, women managers 107, 145
dual-career families 15, 164, 174, 176

early retirement 14, 34, 81, 102, 182
earnings, managers 195–6
educational qualifications, managers studied 196–7
efficiency, organizations 9
elderly parents, caring for 108, 154 n4
elite institutions, higher education 191 n6
emotional commitment, to jobs 144
equal opportunities legislation 117
evaluation stage, careers 81
Evans, P. 132–3
exploratory stage, careers 81
extrinsic rewards, jobs 42, 48, 181

family, priority 97
family relationships 33
  influence of work experiences 130
  subordinated to career 136–7
family responsibilities, division of 157
fatigue 26, 27
female attributes, women managers 135
financial security, jobs as source of 92
Forester, T. 39–40
formal training, managers 30
Francis, A. 35
fringe benefits 49
frustration 26, 27
functional groupings, managers studied 194, 195

gender, job dissatisfaction and 45–7
gender roles 178 n2
geographical mobility, careers and 137, 155, 164–6
goal achievement 57

Handy, C. 158, 176–7
hierarchical nature, bureaucratic organizations 89
high trust relationships 59

INDEX

higher education, elite institutions 191 n6
hobbies 149–50
home
  looking after, women managers 107–9
  as private arena 149
  as refuge 148
home-based pursuits 33
home-work conflicts, women managers 107–9, 110–11
homemakers 178 n1
house moves, career-related 146–8, 164
human aspects, jobs 68
human relations 31, 61
  skills 184
  training in 68, 69
human resource management 184, 187
husband-wife relationships 157

In Search of Excellence 56
in-depth interviews 192
incentive schemes, managers 11
independence, work and non-work 132
independent thought and action 42, 43
industrial relations 8
inflation 8
informal networks 119
information, access to 37
instrumentality, work-leisure patterns 132, 133
interpersonal skills 11, 12, 52 n3, 59–60, 62, 72, 144
interview, in-depth 192
intrinsic rewards, jobs 42, 181

Japanese-owned companies 189
job characteristics, actual and desired 43–4
job enlargement 25
job enrichment 183
job satisfaction 52 n5
  managers 41–8
job threats, new technology 40–1
job-orientation, women 85
jobs
  distancing from 136
  emotional commitment 144
  moves 12
  self-development within 95–6
  series of related 79

junior managers 9, 194–5
  constraints on 22–3
  declining motivation 58
  feelings of exclusion from management 26, 28
  instrumentality of work 142–3
  intrinsic rewards 47
  morale and motivation 75
  reduced promotion prospects 83–4
  spillover 141–2

Kanter, R. M. 111

labour, alienation 153 n1
large-scale organizations 3–4, 192–3
  decentralization 56
  employment within 130
  flexibility 10–11
  growth 1–2
  patriarchal nature 115
leadership
  female style of 121–2, 128 n5
  firm 66
  personal forms 75
  skills 62–3
  women managers 121–2
leadership styles 72, 185–7
  bureaucratic organizations 63–5
  managers 68–71
leisure 33, 149–51, 180, 182
leisure activities, influence of work experiences 130
life satisfactions, managers 97–102
lifestyles
  non-work 180
  non-working 142
living standards, improving 3

male managers
  age groups 193
  attitudes to security 44
  educational qualifications 196–7
  limited importance attached to wife's career 164–6
  personal satisfactions 97, 99–102
  relationships with wives 151–3
manage, right to 65, 188
management
  assertive styles 17 n6, 120, 135
  bureaucratic model 10, 54–5
  exclusion from 26, 28
  functions 21
  polarization 22–3, 38

working-class recruitment 191 n4
management buy-outs 104
management development 184
management hierarchies, reduction in size and extent 10
management styles 3, 66–7, 120
managerial careers, timespan 14
managerial families 155, 156
managerial skills, acquisition 30
managerial tiers, abolition 11
managerial work, nature of 20–2
managers
  age groups 193–4
  anti-organizational attitudes 97
  balance between work and private lives 179
  behaviour 21–2
  career prospects 3
  career-related house moves 146–8
  changing attitudes to careers 82–3
  changing circumstances 2
  earnings 195–6
  educational qualifications 196–7
  emotional relationships 5
  impact of new technology 34–41
  instrumental attitudes to work 13–14
  job satisfaction 41–8
  leadership styles 68–71
  leisure pursuits 149–51
  life satisfactions 97–102
  limited promotion prospects 91–3
  marital status 197
  monitoring 179–80
  partners Chapter 7
  perceptions of factors in career success 87–91
  preferred organizational structures 72–5
  preoccupation with work-related issues during free time 139–46
  pressure on 9, 31–2
  selection for survey 193
  stress 25–6
  traditional careers 79–81
  training 30, 184
  turnround 188–9, 191 n7
  use of term 17 n3
  wives 15, 151–3
  work roles 11–12
  workload 23–5
managers, see also junior managers; senior managers; women managers; male managers; middle managers
manual workers 52 n6
manufacturing enterprises, traditional 188
manufacturing industry, forms of control 76 n4
marital status, managers 197
marriage
  subordinated to career 136–7
  traditional 176–7
married women 128 n3, 178 n1
  career-orientation 123–4
  changing expectations 138
  domestic role 107
  promotion 167, 169
  spillover 145–6
medium-sized companies 56
mental exhaustion 26, 27
mentors, female subordinates 118–19
mid-career crisis 14, 93
middle managers 9, 182, 194–5
  constraints on 22
  control and supervision 12–13
  declining motivation 58
  feelings of exclusion from management 26, 28
  impact of new technology 34–41
  instrumentality of work 142–3
  intrinsic rewards 47
  morale 28–9, 75
  spillover 141–2
mixed economy 7
morale, middle managers 28–9, 75

need hierarchy 42
networks, informal 90
new technology 52 n4, 159–60, 178 n4
  impact on managers 34–41
non-manual occupations, managers' wives 163, 164
non-work, work and 129–33
nuclear family, functional for managerial success 155

occupational careers 12, 87
occupational success, excessive commitment 13
occupations, female managers' partners 168–9
office technology, doubts over 39–41
oil crisis 1973 8
organization men 4

INDEX

organizational acceptability, factor in
  career success 89
organizational behaviour 17 n5
organizational careers 12, 87
organizational cultures 76 n3
organizational structures 72, 76 n2
  changes in, accompanying techno-
    logical change 38–9
  decentralized 9–10, 54–5
  looser 74–5, 144, 180, 188, 189
  managers' preferences 72–5
organizations
  selected for study 192–3
  values and assumptions 53–4
organizing, management function 21
overheads, cutting 9

parental roles 176
parenthood 110–11
partners, women managers 167–76
passive relaxation 149
patriarchal nature, large-scale organizations 115
pay 42, 43
  dissatisfaction with 48–50
pay systems, performance-related
  184–5
performance
  acceptable minimum standard 95
  factor in career success 89
performance indicators, task-related
  22
performance-related incentive schemes
  11
performance-related pay systems
  184–5
performance-related targets 31
personal costs
  career moves 148
  career pursuit 99
personal growth 42, 43, 47
personal identity
  crises 178 n8
  effects of work experiences 133–5
  independent of work 137
  non-work 138
personal lifestyles 82–3
  influence of work experiences 130
  outside work 100
personal relationships 181
  importance 142
  priority 97
  subordinated to career 136–7

personal satisfactions, managers
  97–102
personal skills 31
  lack of acceptable 186
personal status 42
personal success, work-related 80–1
personality types, bureaucratic organizations 54–5
Peters, T. 56
planning, management function 21
post-capitalism 4
private lives, redefinition of character
  153
private sector organizations, non-
  bureaucratic procedures 58–9
professional colleagues, women as 118
professional jobs, lower-grade, managers' wives 163
professional skills, selling back 105 n3
professionals 50–1
professions, working-class recruitment 191 n4
project teams 56, 61
promotion 47, 66, 96, 182, 191 n2
  costs and benefits 137
  emphasis on 79–80
  married women 167, 169
  opportunities 84–5
  prospects 42, 43–4
  reduced prospects 83–4, 91–3
psychological commitment, to work
  131–2
psychological dependence, upon work
  100
psychological immersion, in jobs 55,
  56–7, 75
psychological outcomes, career failure
  93–4
public sector management, as specialist function 7
public sector organizations 161–2,
  192, 193
  forms of control 76 n5
  task-orientated management 58
  women managers 77 n10, 117

questionnaire survey 192, 193

redundancy 180, 181
  managers 10
regional differences, career moves
  147, 148
reliability, factor in career success 89

results, factor in career success 89
retirement 100
retirement age 102
retraining 103
  mid-life 81
role cultures, bureaucratic organizations 57
routine administrative tasks 22, 23, 28

salary surveys 195–6
sales jobs, managers' wives 163, 164
scientific management 51 n1
security 42, 44–5
self-confidence, women managers 135
self-development, within jobs 95–6
self-employment 12, 82, 103–4
self-fulfilment, outside work 84
self-identity, work role and 33–4
self-respect 42
senior management, compatibility
  with 89
senior managers 182–3, 194–5
  autonomy 12–13
  corporate values and ideals 185
  earnings 49
  management styles 64–5
  organizational restructuring 57–9
  spillover 139–40, 143–4
services, selling back 105 n3
short-term objectives 47
single women
  domestic pressures 108
  spillover 145–6
small companies 56
spillover 135, 144
  junior managers 141–2
  middle managers 141–2
  senior managers 139–40, 143–4
  women managers 135–6, 144–6
  work and non-work 132–3
staff appraisal schemes 105 n4
staff reductions 25
staff supervision 31
staff training 56–7
state intervention 3–4, 7
stereotyping, women managers 111,
  115–16
strategic decision-making 28
stress 25–6, 52 n2
  impact of new technology 36–7
subordinates, working autonomy
  60–1
success, ambiguous attitudes to 182

supervision
  changing styles 35
  firm 64–5

takeovers 10
targets, pressure to meet 47–8
task forces 61
task-related ideals 57–8, 59, 81
technological change, consequences
  38–9
technostructures 4, 7
television, watching 149
time, for children 173–4
tokens, women as 111
trade unionism, technical, scientific
  and management staffs 28
trade unions 8
training, managers 30, 184
trustworthiness, factor in career
  success 89, 90

unskilled jobs, fall in 35

visibility, women 111, 112–13
voluntary severance schemes 34

Waterman, R. 56
welfare state, growth of 6–7
white collar workers 52 n6
wives
  bankers 178 n5
  career opportunities 164–6
  involvement with husbands' job
    158–62
  managers 5–6, 15, 93
  managers' relationships with 151–3
  role as homemakers 156
  support in careers 155
  vicarious careers 156–7
  working 162–7, 177
women, expectations about employment 15
women managers 16, 106
  age groups 193–4
  assertiveness and self-confidence
    135
  attitudes to security 44–5
  career patterns 85–7, 109–11
  career success 67–8, 89–91
  career-orientation 123–5
  children 172–4
  educational qualifications 196–7
  job dissatisfaction 45–7

INDEX

junior and middle-level positions
190
leadership 121–2
partners 167–76
personal satisfactions 97–9
preferred organizational structures
72–4
pressures 106–9
public sector organizations 77 n10,
117
relationships with male colleagues
111–16
spillover 135–6, 144–6
subordinates 119–20
work and non-work 131
work orientations 183
women's movement 15, 157
work
instrumental attitudes to 33–4,
96–7, 136, 142–3, 149
non-work and 129–33
psychological dependence upon 100
psychological and emotional
distance 191 n1

self-fulfilment outside 150–1, 153
wives involvement with husband's
158–62
work ethic 180
work experiences
effects on personal identity 133–5
women, unpredictable nature 85–6
work role, separation from self-
identity 33–4
work roles, managers 11–12
work-related issues, preoccupation
with, during free time 139–46
work-related tensions, release at home
33
workaholics 180
working autonomy, subordinates
60–1
working life, quality of 153 n2
working practices, creative 55
working week, length of 23, 24
working wives 162–7
workload, managers 23–5
workplace, control 8